To

From

Date

STORIES
OF
Friendship
TO WARM THE HEART

STORIES OF
Friendship
TO WARM THE HEART

True Stories of Hope and Inspiration

Guideposts

New York

Stories of Friendship to Warm the Heart

ISBN-10: 0-8249-3217-X
ISBN-13: 978-0-8249-3217-6

Published by Guideposts
16 East 34th Street
New York, New York 10016
Guideposts.org

Distributed by Ideals Publications, a Guideposts company
2630 Elm Hill Pike, Suite 100
Nashville, Tennessee 37214

Guideposts and *Ideals* are registered trademarks of Guideposts.

Acknowledgments

Every attempt has been made to credit the sources of copyrighted material used in this book. If any such acknowledgment has been inadvertently omitted or miscredited, receipt of such information would be appreciated.

Scripture quotations marked (KJV) are taken from *The King James Version of the Bible.*

Scripture quotations marked (NIV) are taken from *The Holy Bible, New International Version.* Copyright © 1973, 1978, 1984, 2011 by Biblica, Inc. Used by permission of Zondervan. All rights reserved worldwide. www.zondervan.com

Scripture quotations marked (NLT) are from the *Holy Bible, New Living Translation.* Copyright © 1996, 2004, 2007 by Tyndale House Foundation. Used by permission of Tyndale House Publishers Inc., Carol Stream, Illinois 60188. All rights reserved.

Scripture quotations marked (PHILLIPS) are taken from *The New Testament in Modern English,* copyright © 1958, 1959, 1960 J. B. Phillips and 1947, 1952, 1955, 1957 the MacMillan Company, New York. Used by permission. All rights reserved.

Cover and interior design by Thinkpen Design, Inc. | www.thinkpendesign.com
Typeset by Aptara, Inc.

Printed and bound in China
10 9 8 7 6 5 4 3 2 1

Contents

Introduction

A listening ear when we feel the world has tuned us out. A kind word when harsh treatment has worn deeply at our souls. A hand to hold on to when we feel like letting go. Someone to rejoice with us when our joy is overflowing....Friendship is deeply meaningful to the human experience. Many a downtrodden soul has been buoyed by the strong hand of a friend. Many a peril has been avoided by the wise words of a partner. Many a joy has been doubled by the smile of a loved one.

The Bible has told us, and our spirits bear witness, that we were never intended to live this life alone. Man, truly, is not an island. We depend on each other, in the good times and the bad, to provide strength, wisdom, and encouragement.

May the true accounts contained in this volume remind you of the gift from above known as friendship. And may you be inspired to invest more deeply in all the different kinds of friendships in your own life, big and small, new and old. As Proverbs 27:17 (NIV) tells us, iron sharpens iron, so one person sharpens another.

Best Friends Forever

BY JUDY LOGGIA

My ten-year-old, Donna, burst through the front door.

"Mom, I made a new friend at school today," she said. "Can she come over tomorrow?"

Donna was a shy kid, and I had been praying for her to make some friends to bring her out of her shell.

"Sure, honey, that sounds great," I said, thinking back to my own best friend growing up.

Lillian and I lived across the street from each other in Washington Heights, New York. We met at age ten too, and were instantly joined at the hip. Like my daughter, I was introverted, but Lillian drew me out and boosted my confidence. She was one of the friendliest people in school. And beautiful too—with shiny black hair, so glossy it was almost indigo, and a mile-wide smile. I knew we would be best friends forever.

During our senior year of high school, Lillian went on a trip to Florida, the first time we'd be apart for more than

1

a few days. "I'll be back soon," she told me. But three days later I answered my door to find Lillian's sister standing there, a pall across her face. "Judy...Lillian's..." She could hardly get the words out. My best friend had drowned on vacation.

Shortly afterward, my family moved to New Jersey. Over the years I lost touch with Lillian's family. But I still thought of her often. Tears formed in my eyes whenever I did. *What I wouldn't give to feel close to her again.*

The next day Donna brought her new friend home. "Hi, Mrs. Loggia," the little girl said, skipping through the front door. She flipped her hair from her shoulders—hair so shiny and black it was almost indigo. She shot me a giant smile. "My name's Lillian."

That hair. That smile. Lillian. How wonderful—my daughter's new friend was so much like the best friend I had lost.

I was still dizzy from the similarities when Lillian's mom came by to pick her up later that afternoon. I opened the door to let her in.

"Judy!" she screamed. Before I knew it, her arms had wrapped me in a tight hug. Pretty friendly for someone I had never met! "It's me," she said, laughing. "Lillian's sister, from Washington Heights."

Yes, my daughter's friend looked familiar all right. She was Lillian's niece. Her namesake.

> *One's life has value so long*
> *as one attributes value to the life of others,*
> *by means of love, friendship, and compassion.*
>
> SIMONE DE BEAUVOIR

I'll Never Forget You... Laura Benét

BY SHARON LINNEA

I came to New York one year, fresh from Missouri, to finish school at New York University. What I had no way of knowing when I arrived was how much my real education would have to do with Laura.

She came into my life one autumn day on a number three bus that rumbled down Fifth Avenue. As the bus stopped at Twelfth Street to discharge passengers, one elderly woman was having trouble negotiating the last long step to the ground. Most of us just sat and watched, but a voice right behind me barked, "Young man, this is a kneeling bus. Would you be kind enough to let it kneel?"

The driver, put out, lowered the bus step. The sturdy voice behind me, it turned out, belonged to another older woman. She got up and helped the first lady off the bus.

"Don't be afraid to speak up for yourself," I heard her say. I had to smile—she herself was eighty if she was a day.

I ran into her again one Friday in an Eighth Street deli. Her eyesight was poor, and she was having trouble counting change to pay for her purchase.

"Here, ma'am, this is what you need," I said, laying out the quarters. She thanked me and was off.

The next time I saw her she was struggling with a large package. I offered to help. As we walked, we chatted a bit. I discovered that her name was Laura and her apartment hotel was only two blocks from my dormitory in Greenwich Village. She was cautious, she said, and sorry, but she couldn't let a stranger come up to her room.

In the next weeks and months I kept running into her, and a crazy-quilt kind of relationship began to form through these odd meetings and patches of conversation. Eventually we met for dinner at a local restaurant. She seemed genuinely interested in my plans to be a writer; I felt I'd done a lonely old lady a good turn.

Then one winter day Laura invited me up to her small apartment. It was a homey studio, crammed with books (from which old newspaper clippings were forever escaping), boxes of letters, poetry magazines.

She'd brought up her mail and she handed me a poetry magazine. "I can't quite read it," she said. "Have I anything in this one?"

Laura—a poet? I looked at the contents on the brown cover and, to my surprise, there was her name. "Why, yes, you do," I said. "'February Light.'"

A satisfied smile crossed her face as she sat at her small writing desk in the afternoon light—and recited the entire poem from memory.

My amazement had just begun. As I took the magazine to the shelf, I saw a copy of *King David*—by beloved American bard Stephen Vincent Benét—which had won *The Nation*'s prize for poetry. The gold-embossed volume, inscribed by Benét to his parents, was copy number one, the very first to roll off the presses, back in 1923.

"Laura," I asked, "how did you come by this?"

She answered simply, "Why, Tibbie was my baby brother."

Laura was Stephen Vincent Benét's older—that's right, *older*—sister. She'd just turned ninety-two.

She sensed my astonishment, and her eyes danced merrily.

"My dear," she said, "you must always give people room to surprise you. If you don't, they'll probably act like the boring people you expect them to be. You must give God room to surprise you too!"

As it turned out, Laura was full of surprises.

She had plenty of pluck, though her body was failing. She'd sometimes call me at inopportune times, an edge of panic in her voice: "There's a bill here I can't quite read. It seems important—what am I to do?"

"Oh, Laura," I'd sigh, seeing my Saturday afternoon slip away. But I'd go over to read the mail to her and to put her bills and checks in order. We'd start to talk, and then to laugh. And Laura would surprise me again. How much those eyes, glossy now with cataracts, had seen. She wove wonderful stories of people and places in decades—in a century—I never knew. I began to learn more about the literary world from this older woman, with her soft, braided hair and "proper" hats, than from any star professor.

In the 1930s the Benéts were one of America's foremost literary families. Stephen, best known for the poem "John Brown's Body" and the tale *The Devil and Daniel Webster*, was a two-time Pulitzer Prize winner. His older brother, William Rose Benét, was a poet, an essayist, and an editor; William's wife, Elinor Wylie, was a brilliant poet.

Laura herself had more than ten books to her name: biographies, children's books, poems. She'd also trained as a social worker at the turn of the century, putting in selfless years at Manhattan's now historic Spring Street Settlement.

"God takes care of us," she'd tell me, "and He expects us to take care of one another." Laura's faith was important to her, and she never missed a Sunday at church.

It was a great lesson to hear Laura talk about writers she'd known. "Willie and Elinor used to host splendid dinner parties," she would say. "In those days they called them *coteries*." Evidently Laura had turned up at these parties unexpectedly on more than one occasion to alert the self-absorbed literati to the world outside: unsanitary conditions in the tenements of the East Village, or hungry children in the Bronx. "Willie was often put out with me," she concluded with a satisfied chuckle.

Yes, Laura was full of surprises.

Like any beginning writer, I was afraid of failure. "Oh, Laura," I'd complain, "Lanford Wilson's from my home state. He's a famous playwright. He's in all the papers. I'll never amount to anything."

"Dear," she said sharply, "you've got to decide. Do you want to be a writer or a celebrity? They're very different things. Take Scott Fitzgerald: He was a good writer when he put his mind to it. But when he was busy being a celebrity, he was the silliest man I ever saw.

"What God asks of us is to be craftsmen, investing our talents, returning to the same tasks day after day, always trying a little harder. In our work and in our lives."

In relationships too, Laura surprised me. In a city where friendships seemed to last only a season, or long enough to serve a purpose, Laura had friendships that spanned two world wars. She and a girlhood friend still exchanged rollicking letters, often assuming the character of imaginary alter egos whose adventures, amorous and otherwise, still spanned the globe. The women were always honest with each other and often disagreed, but their friendship had obviously been deepened by hard times.

Despite our seventy-four-year age difference, Laura insisted on calling me Little Sister. For college graduation, she surprised me once again. She'd arranged for an old friend to take her to a store way uptown so that she could choose my gift herself. As I opened the box, she said anxiously, "The salesgirl said a young person would like this...."

That necklace meant as much as any diploma.

As time passed, I became more worried about Laura. I prayed that she wouldn't be left alone in time of crisis. Then one summer Sunday morning our churches were meeting together, but Laura wasn't there. After the service I rushed to her building. One look at the building manager's face and I knew my fears were well-founded.

Laura had had a heart attack alone in her room the night before. She'd fallen and broken her hip. Unable to crawl to the phone, she'd lain on the floor all night long.

"We found her this morning," the manager said. "She's in the hospital now."

I ran to St. Vincent's Hospital. A heart attack. She'd been alone, in pain, all night. When the nurse at the admitting desk said, "Are you family?" I said yes without thinking twice.

In the cardiac unit's intensive care wing, I took Laura's hand and said, "Laura, I love you. I'm so sorry, so sorry you were alone."

Laura looked at me and shook her head. "But I wasn't alone, Little Sister. There was a man with me, a young man. It was dark, so I couldn't even see if he was black or white. He said, 'Laura, when I'm in trouble or afraid, I pray to the Lord.' So he held my hand, and we prayed and sang hymns together all night."

I was about to say, "But there couldn't have been a man. The manager said your door was locked from the inside." Instead I remembered praying that Laura wouldn't be alone in time of crisis. And I knew what Laura always said was true: "God takes care of us." With a smile I remembered what else she said: "You must give God room to surprise you."

Laura wasn't able to return to her apartment. She moved into the Village Nursing Home, which was in the same neighborhood. She sorely missed being on her own but did her best to accept the help she now needed.

One Saturday a couple of years later I met a friend for lunch. Suddenly, without knowing why, I pushed my chair back from my half-eaten sandwich and stood up. "It's great seeing you," I said, "but I have to go." My friend couldn't have been more surprised than I as I put on my coat, left money for the check, and hurried into the winter streets.

At the nursing home I took the steps by twos. When I reached Laura's room, I knew why I'd been "sent for."

Laura was breathing with the help of an oxygen mask. The nurse by the bed motioned for me to come close. "I love you, Laura," I whispered. My fingers brushed silky gray hair from her forehead as those wise eyes closed for the last time. Holding her still-warm hand, I heard the nurse beside me softly quoting the Twenty-third Psalm. We finished the verses together.

It was hard to leave the nursing home that evening; I didn't want to leave Laura behind. Yet as I stood on the steps looking over the village square, the hurrying people, the honking traffic, something started to change. I suddenly saw before me the world as Laura had seen it every day of her ninety-six years: a world of wonder . . . poets . . . angels. A world in which one's life could change on a number three bus traveling down Fifth Avenue.

I started down the steps, not knowing what surprises lay ahead, from people and from God. But thanks to Laura, I knew I would be ready.

No love, no friendship, can cross the path of our destiny without leaving some mark on it forever.

FRANÇOIS MAURIAC

The Truest of Friends

BY NANCY SULLIVAN GENG

I pulled the pink envelope from our mailbox just as my daughter was coming home from school. It looked like a birthday party invitation. "SARAH" was carefully printed in bold, black letters. When Sarah stepped off the bus I tucked the envelope into her hand. "It's...it's...for me," she stuttered, delighted.

In the unseasonably warm February sun we sat down on the front porch. As I helped her open the envelope, I wondered who had sent it. Maybe Emily or perhaps Michael, pals from her special-education class.

"It's...it's...from Maranda!" Sarah said, pointing to the front of the card. There, framed with hearts, was a photo of a girl I had never seen before. She had beautiful long hair, a dimpled grin, and warm smiling eyes. "Maranda is eight years old," the caption read. "Come and celebrate on Valentine's Day."

Glancing at the picture, I felt uneasy. Clearly, Maranda was not handicapped. Sarah, on the other hand, had Down syndrome and was developmentally delayed in all areas. At age nine she still functioned on a preschool level. Her disability was obvious, marked by a hearing aid, stuttering, and glasses with thick lenses.

A happy child, she had many friends who used wheelchairs and braces and walkers. But this was the first time she had been invited to the home of a nondisabled child. "How did you meet Maranda?" I asked.

"At...at...school. We eat lunch together every... every day."

Even though Sarah was in special education, she socialized with other second graders during gym, lunch, and homeroom. I had always hoped she would make friends outside her program. Why, then, did I feel apprehensive?

Because I'm her mother, I thought. I loved Sarah. I wanted and prayed that she would have the best. I also knew a friendship with Sarah called for extra sensitivity, tolerance, and understanding. Was the child in the photo capable of that?

Valentine's Day came. Sarah dressed in her favorite pink lace dress and white patent leather shoes. As we drove to Maranda's party she sat next to me in the front seat, clutching the Barbie doll she had wrapped with Winnie-the-Pooh paper and masking tape. "I...I'm so excited," she said.

I smiled, but deep inside I felt hesitant. There would be other children at the party. Would they tease Sarah? Would Maranda be embarrassed in front of her other friends? *Please, Lord*, I prayed, *don't let Sarah get hurt*.

I pulled into the driveway of a house decorated with silver heart-shaped balloons. Waiting at the front door was a little girl in a red sweater trimmed with ribboned hearts. It was Maranda. "Sarah's here!" she called. Racing to our car, she welcomed my daughter with a wraparound hug. Soon seven giggling girls followed Maranda's lead, welcoming Sarah with smiles.

"Bye, Mom," Sarah said, waving as she and the others ran laughing into the house. Maranda's mother, Mary, greeted me at my rolled-down car window.

"Thanks for bringing Sarah," she said. "Maranda is so excited Sarah could come to her party." Mary went on to explain that her daughter was an only child and that Maranda and Sarah had become special friends at school. "Maranda talks about her all the time," she said.

I drove away, amazed. Still, I couldn't get over my uneasiness. Could this friendship ever be equal? Maranda would need to learn the language of Sarah's speech. She would need patience when Sarah struggled with certain tasks. That was a lot to ask of an eight-year-old.

As the months passed I watched the girls' friendship grow. They spent many hours together in our home. Fixing dinner in the kitchen, I heard giggles fill the family room as they twirled around an old recliner or watched *The Lion King*. Other times they dressed up in my old hats and outdated blouses, pretending to be famous singers. Soon the months turned to years.

One afternoon in late autumn, I watched the two of them sitting next to each other at our kitchen table. Sarah held a pencil; Maranda had a tablet of paper.

Maranda called out each letter as she guided Sarah's hand: "S-A-R-A-H." Though some of the letters had been printed backward or upside-down, Maranda praised Sarah's effort. "Great job," she said, applauding.

At Christmastime the girls exchanged gifts. Sarah gave Maranda a photograph of herself, a framed First Communion picture. "You look beautiful," Maranda said as she admired Sarah's white ruffled dress and long lace veil. In return, Maranda gave Sarah a gray-flannel elephant trimmed with an "I Love You" tag. It quickly became Sarah's favorite stuffed animal, and she slept with it every night.

A few weeks into the new year Sarah came home from school looking downcast. "M–Maranda is…is sick," she said. I thought maybe she had caught the bug circulating at school. Minutes later, however, Sarah's special-education teacher called. Maranda was in the hospital. She had a seizure at school and was diagnosed with a brain tumor. Surgeons performed a risky operation, which had left

Maranda paralyzed on one side with impaired speech and vision. The biopsy results weren't back yet.

"Can we visit her?" I asked. I knew Sarah would want to see her friend.

"Maranda is very despondent and not up to seeing anybody," the teacher told me. "Her parents are requesting cards rather than visits."

"We'll keep her in our prayers," I promised.

That night Sarah knelt beside her bed, clutching her stuffed elephant. "Please ma...ma...make Maranda better," she prayed. Night after night she implored God to heal her friend. Then one night in early February Sarah stopped abruptly in the middle of her prayer. She nudged me.

"Let's ma...ma...make a valentine for Ma...Maranda."

The next day we sat together at the kitchen table as I helped Sarah write Maranda's name on a large sheet of pink-and-white construction paper. She decorated each letter with stickers and glittery Magic Markers. She drew a large heart around the name, then glued candy hearts with phrases like "Friends Forever" and "Be Mine" on them. In similar fashion she added four more pages. Just before we slid the card into a large envelope, Sarah asked, "How...how...how do I spell *love*?" I called out the letters as she painstakingly printed "LOVE," the letters crooked and out of place, followed by her name.

Two weeks passed. We heard that Maranda had additional surgery. On Valentine's Day, I got a phone call from her mother. "Maranda's home," she said, "and wants to see Sarah."

"Home?" I asked with surprise.

"Maranda's tumor was benign. We're hoping for a full recovery."

As we discussed Maranda's prognosis, she relayed how thankful she was for Sarah and her card. "Maranda was very depressed. She had stacks of letters, cards, and gifts, but wouldn't open any of them. Then one morning Sarah's homemade card arrived. We opened it, and Maranda burst into a huge smile. She hugged it and wouldn't put it down." Mary's voice was choked with emotion. "It was an answer to prayer."

I realized then that Sarah and Maranda were the truest of friends. Their bond was defined not by intellect or health or handicap, but by love, unconditionally given and received. They had overcome disability with laughter and support. Their friendship had always been equal.

Today both girls are doing well. Maranda is almost twelve, and Sarah is going on thirteen. With the help of intensive therapy Maranda's neurological functions returned to normal, and Sarah's speech has improved immensely. She can even read some. Though we've moved to a different neighborhood, the girls still keep in touch. Recently Maranda came to sleep over.

As the girls sat at our kitchen table they talked about Maranda's newly pierced ears and Sarah's "secret" boyfriend from her special-ed class. Then in the middle of their conversation Sarah opened a kitchen drawer and pulled out a tablet and pencil.

"S-A-R-A-H," Maranda called out, just like old times. As Sarah printed her name without any help, Maranda looked on and clapped. "Great job, Sarah!" she said. I took a peek at my daughter's masterpiece. Her name had been written perfectly.

> *The most I can do for my friend is simply to be his friend. I have no wealth to bestow on him. If he knows that I am happy in loving him, he will want no other reward. Is not friendship divine in this?*
>
> HENRY DAVID THOREAU

The Power of Love

BY YOLANDA MARIE ADAMS

B y the time I was ten, I'd known so much difficulty in my life that the taunts of the other kids at school shouldn't have stung. But their cruelty cut me deeply, leaving a hurt that wouldn't go away.

"Jingle Bells, Yolanda smells!" "That's 'cause she doesn't wash her hair." One autumn afternoon the insults got to be too much, maybe because I knew there was some truth to them. I ran from the playground, my ratty old sneakers slap-slapping on the pavement. "That's right," one boy yelled, "go home to the crazy lady!"

I turned onto my street, my footsteps slowing. Where was I running to? It wasn't as if our house were any sort of refuge. I stopped in front of the two prettiest houses on the block. They looked as neat and well cared for as the two girls I'd seen step out their front doors to walk side by side to school together. *It's not as if I have a place like one of those to go home to,* I thought. *Not anymore.*

Once I, too, had lived in a cozy home with parents who loved me—a few years earlier, in Los Angeles. Dad had worked hard to provide for us and so had Mom, but she always made time to sit me on her lap and sing to me. Nothing, in those days, had seemed more beautiful to me than my mother's voice.

Then my great-grandmother and great-aunt fell ill. Looking after them and my brothers and sisters and me, Mom got overloaded. I guess she broke. One day she was taken away to the state hospital. Years later I found out she'd been subjected to massive electroshock and drug therapy, but all I knew then was that when she came back, she wasn't Mom. Gone were the sweet songs, swallowed up by babbling that could escalate, without warning, into shouting.

Dad had moved our family here to La Puente, California, when I was eight, thinking the small-town atmosphere would be easier on Mom. But she hadn't gotten any better. She'd stay parked on the couch for hours, staring blankly at the TV, ignoring the dirty laundry and dishes. Those were her good days. On her bad days, she'd go outside without clothes on, yelling at anyone who tried to come near. Even with the long hours he put in at the sheriff's department, Dad couldn't afford a full-time babysitter for us kids. So whenever Mom went into the hospital, we were sent to stay with various relatives in south-central Los Angeles.

Between all those different homes, I never really fit in anywhere. At school I was a loner, a convenient target for the other kids to pick on. I learned that grown-ups couldn't protect me. I had to hide within myself, to withdraw into a kind of box where nothing could touch me.

Wanting to slip into that hiding place again, out of reach of those playground taunts, I turned away from the pretty houses and resignedly started for my own. "Hey, wait up!" I heard someone call from down the street. Two sets of footsteps quickened behind me. Probably kids wanting to tease me. I picked up my pace. "Please, Yolanda?" I chanced a glance over my shoulder.

Behind me were the two girls who lived in those houses I'd been admiring. They looked so perfect in their dresses, hair ribbons, and shiny leather shoes, it made me feel more ashamed than ever about my uncombed hair and way-too-long-unwashed clothes. I ran inside, past my mom on the couch, to my bedroom.

The next morning on my walk to school, the same two girls fell in step beside me. "I'm Terrie Silva," said the dark-haired one, her eyes as sparkly as her glasses. "And that's Debbie Powell."

"Hi," the blonde girl said softly. I was so stunned they weren't backing away from me that I couldn't say a word.

"We've seen you around," Terrie said. Then, her gaze locking on mine, she announced, "We're going to be your friends."

Not once in the years I'd been shuttling between LA and La Puente had someone said anything like that to me. Was this a trick? What were they up to?

Pretty soon I found out. Wherever I went from then on, Debbie and Terrie were with me. Walking to school, in the hallways, in the cafeteria, at recess, I wasn't alone anymore. The kids on the playground still jeered, even at Terrie and Debbie. "Why are you hanging out with Stinky?" I'd hang my head, wishing I could disappear. But Debbie would tuck her arm in mine, and Terrie would declare boldly, "Her name is Yolanda. And she's our friend."

There was that word again. *Friend*. It had been so long since I'd had one, I had forgotten what it was like. I sensed that what Terrie and Debbie were offering me was good, but I didn't really understand how to accept it. Still, it was hard to resist their determined efforts. When Terrie had Debbie and me over to make oatmeal cookies, and Mrs. Silva welcomed me with a hug, for a moment it was like I was part of a real family again. The next week we went to Debbie's to bake chocolate chip cookies. And Debbie's mom was just as sweet as she was.

When I started going to church with Terrie and Debbie and their parents, I noticed the sidelong glances and whispers from some of the other parishioners. Was it because I was the only black person there? Or because my clothes were shabby? I cringed in the pew, the walls of my box beginning to close in on me again. Then the pastor, Reverend Kutz, came and shook my hand. "Don't mind those people," he told me. "They don't know who you are. But God in His love does, and together we will teach the others."

Though I wasn't quite sure what the pastor meant, the kindness in his voice reached through my hurt and shame. I sat up a little straighter. When he asked if I'd like to come to Sunday school, I said yes. I liked the teacher, Mrs. Fike. She treated me as if I were someone special.

One rainy afternoon about a year after they had sought me out, Debbie and Terrie were walking me home. We were almost at my house when my mom ran out at us in a rage. "Mom, don't," I pleaded. She ignored me. "Go away!" Mom screamed at Debbie and Terrie. "And don't come back. No one wants you here!"

Terrified, they took off. Mom pushed me inside and slammed the door. I felt shut in so tight I could hardly breathe.

Later, my mother dozed off in front of the TV, and I was finally able to slip out. But I only got as far as the edge of the street. *Where can I go?* I thought, sinking down on the curb. *Debbie and Terrie won't want anything to do with me now.*

I watched the rainwater go by in the gutter, wishing I could be swept down the drain with it. *What's the point?* I asked myself. *Mom chased away the only thing in my life that was good.*

The next morning Debbie and Terrie were waiting to walk to school with me. "I didn't think you'd be back," I said. "Not after my mom—"

"We're your friends," Debbie said. Terrie added, "No matter what." I took their outstretched hands, but I knew I didn't deserve their friendship.

Then one Sunday the children's sermon really spoke to me. "Jesus loves you. You don't have to be perfect. He won't give up on you, no matter what."

Like Terrie and Debbie? I thought, glancing at them on either side of me.

"He loves you so much that He will bear your hurt and sorrow for you. You just have to open your heart to Him."

I stared up at the figure in the stained-glass window above the altar. Then I bowed my head. "Please, Jesus, I need You," I whispered.

All at once, from that figure above came an outpouring so intense that momentarily everything else—including the troubles in my life—faded. Was this what Jesus' love felt like? It was even better than walking to school with Debbie and Terrie, or sitting on Mom's lap way back when and hearing her sweet voice. This was love sweeter than anything.

For the first time since Mom got sick, I felt there was hope, and even though we continued to struggle, I never let go of it. The nails in Jesus' hands and feet had opened the box I was in, freeing me at last to become the person He and my friends knew I could be.

There have been many miracles in my life—graduating high school and college; becoming a teacher; living through lupus; meeting Paul, with whom I've built a marriage that's twenty-three years strong; raising a happy, healthy family together. Yet the greatest, the one that made all the others possible, was the miracle of God's love, which He first brought home to me through the friendship of two little girls named Terrie and Debbie.

Can we find a friend so faithful who will all our sorrows share? Jesus knows our every weakness; take it to the Lord in prayer.

JOSEPH M. SCRIVEN

What Is Given

BY DAVID WESTERFIELD

Children raced up to the car, trying to sell us melons and bananas. Adults had turned the street into a marketplace, lining the sidewalks with art and trinkets. I was in the African nation of Cameroon with three of my coworkers, and we were headed west, into a remote region of the country. The highway deteriorated into rutted dirt roads. The lush landscape, full of exotic birds, plants, trees, and all kinds of animals, bounced by. Hours later, we came to a stop in a tiny village made up of adobe bricks. There we were greeted by the chiefs of Batseng'la, Bawouwoua, Baletet, Baghonto, and Fokamezo. These villages had been at war, but now the five chiefs wanted good relationships among their people. They had invited us to come to help them.

We'd heard about these five chiefs from Valentin Miafo-Donfack. He left Cameroon to study in the United States and ended up joining the staff of the Shreveport-Bossier Community Renewal program. We're a group of people who try to bring help and hope to all communities by connecting caring people who can improve education, housing, and health care. Most important, we help build friendships. "Friendship," said our founder, Mack McCarter, "is the most powerful force of transformation in the universe."

Valentin believed that the power of friendship could help change his homeland. Cameroon, he told us, was one of the most prosperous nations in all of Africa, thanks to large offshore oil deposits. But, because of corrupt businessmen and politicians, that wealth does not trickle down to the people, the vast majority of whom live in rural areas.

I experienced the shock of seeing abject poverty firsthand. None of these villages had running water; the women walked for miles every day to creeks or wells, carrying battered, leaky buckets. Electricity is a rare luxury. And a typical day's earnings was about forty-five cents.

We spent a week there, talking about how community renewal worked. Before we left, we signed a compact with the chiefs, promising assistance in building a "friendship house" and a training center where they could learn how to work together.

Back in Shreveport, I often wondered about and prayed for the five chiefs. About their people and the incredible hardships they suffered daily. About how lucky we were to live in Louisiana. Then came Hurricane Katrina five months later, and the destruction and terrible suffering.

We got an urgent message from Cameroon. Our friends had seen pictures of the hurricane damage. They feared for our lives, not knowing that Shreveport is five hours north of New Orleans.

We got word back to them that we were all okay.

Not long after that, we heard from them again. The five chiefs had spread the news of what had happened. Some three thousand villagers scraped together whatever they could.

One boy, nine-year-old Bernard Ngimfack, had spent two months working to make enough money for school supplies. "When the chief showed the pictures of Louisiana on the village television," he said, "I gave. Those people had come to my school, and they were very kind to us." Bernard donated twenty-five cents from his savings.

Small gifts such as that added up—the villagers had raised $865. In rural Cameroon, that is truly a small fortune.

The five chiefs wanted to deliver it personally. Churches and other donors stepped forward to pay their airfare. "You came to see our community and help us," one chief said when we met them at the airport. "Now it is our turn to come and show you our friendship." He presented a hand-carved wooden box. Inside was their gift.

We took the chiefs down to New Orleans, where we were met by a group of National Guardsmen. It was surreal. The Lower Ninth Ward—what was left of it—was eerily quiet. Houses washed from their foundations, cars upside down, rubble everywhere. The neighborhood had been abandoned, forgotten. And walking through it all were soldiers in uniform and five Cameroonian chiefs in their colorful native clothes.

The chiefs absorbed it in somber silence. At first I wondered what they were thinking. Then I remembered my visit to their country, the shock I'd felt at seeing how the people lived. And I knew that they understood more deeply than perhaps anyone.

We stopped a couple of blocks from where the Industrial Canal levee had breached. That's when we finally saw someone. A man came up to us and, out of curiosity, wanted to know what we were doing there.

We told him that the five chiefs had come all the way from Africa.

"Wow! I'm from Biloxi, Mississippi, and I thought that was a long way to come," he said. He asked to talk to the chiefs. They told him why they had come. Immediately he shoved his hand into his pocket, fished around and pulled out a twenty-dollar bill. He dug some more. Another twenty. Then a ten. "Please," he said, handing the money to one of the chiefs, "take this to help your people. Let them know how much their gift means to us here." And then he walked away.

Later, the leader of the National Guardsmen asked us all to gather around. "That little boy, giving up part of his school money to help, well…that got to us," he said. "Me and the guys here want to give too. Take this to help your children get the supplies they need." He handed over several hundred dollars to one of the chiefs.

Just before the chiefs went back to Cameroon, we threw them a party.

One of them asked if he could make an announcement. "We are here because of you and we now form one family," he said, receiving loud applause. "We are brothers and sisters. We believe in friendship. We believe in a world where life can be better for every human being." The chiefs and their people, he said, now call their five villages Doumbouo, which means "a meeting place; somewhere people can come together."

We had given to the five chiefs. And they had given back to us. A stranger from Biloxi—who knows what he had lost in the hurricane—gave out of his pocket. National Guardsmen, locals just back from Iraq, gave too. It didn't even matter how much. It wasn't about the money. It was about the bond, the irresistible human urge to help and to hope.

It was also about friendship, the most powerful force of transformation in the whole universe.

Scatter seeds of kindness everywhere you go....
Gather buds of friendship; Keep them till
full-blown; You will find more happiness than
you have ever known.

AMY R. RAABE

The House That Love Built

BY GEORGE VAN INWEGEN

L ike a couple of million other ex-servicemen, I had one consuming dream at the end of World War II: I wanted a family and my own home.

Also, as with a million other guys, the end of the war brought the beginning of a lot of new struggles. First came the long effort to get my discharge; then to find a job, then to earn enough to be married. Finally, I had to find a place to live.

I took a job as a linesman in the telephone company, which made it possible for Bernice and me to be married. The housing situation in Suffern, New York, was no better than in any other community. We were finally lucky enough to establish ourselves in a tiny set of rooms on a nearby estate in what was formerly a chauffeur's apartment over a garage.

"It's yours, if you want to fix it up," I was told. I fixed it up. But we still dreamed of having our own home.

One day I found the property I wanted: a beautiful piece of land with a gurgling brook, trees, and plenty of space where our kids, Jeddie and April, could play. I bought it with what was left of my service savings.

We had land but no means to have a house built. I figured out a way to buy the materials and build one myself, with the help of my father-in-law, Harry Conklin, who was a contractor.

In the summer of 1947, I started to work on the house in my spare time. Every load of dirt carted off, every cinder block set was part of a long-felt dream fitting into place. It was exciting but slow work. By September 11, 1948, only the foundation had been laid.

On this unforgettable Saturday I set aside most of the day to work on the house. First, I picked up a batch of window frames. Later, while climbing a ladder, I noticed a stiffness in my legs. I dismissed it, thinking I had caught a cold.

On Sunday I felt worse.

Monday I was paralyzed.

Tuesday they took me to the hospital.

The diagnosis was like a punch right on the nose. I had polio—a bad case. One leg was useless and the other almost so. Lying on my hospital cot, I felt completely whipped and thoroughly bitter. My past problems and struggles came to my mind and seemed insignificant compared with what faced me now. Doctors were vague when I asked them if I would walk again.

"Your will to get well is about as important as any treatment we can give you," they told me. Yet I wondered if it was worth the effort.

What had I done to deserve such disaster? I asked myself bitterly, just as thousands of others before me have asked when tragedy hits. How could God rob a willing guy of the power to work, a family of a protector and provider? I was licked, with no urge to live.

Later, I found out what happened the day after I was taken to the hospital. My buddies in the maintenance department met that morning in the garage where the phone trucks were stored. Harold Conover, one of my closest friends, told them of my bad luck. They decided they wanted to help me.

What happened from there was the best shot in the arm a discouraged guy possibly could have received.

The ball started to roll when a local contractor, Anthony Cucolo, ran an ad in the *Ramapo Valley Independent*. "Let's Finish the Job," it was titled, and the story told of a fund being started to complete the house that I had started. A committee of prominent businessmen was established to give the fund backing. A miniature model of the house was built in the form of a booth where residents of the town, which only had a population of four thousand, could contribute.

Newspapers and radio stations picked up the story and gave it momentum. The Electrical Workers Union offered skilled workers to complete electrical installations. The Carpenters Union offered to furnish all carpentry work. The Painters Union offered fifteen men to paint the house inside and out. All this without cost.

When the first batch of volunteers arrived to work on the Saturday following my illness, partitions were erected, window frames were installed, the building was partly enclosed, and the roof and roofing were on. A schedule of future work hours, with names of the men who were assigned to toil, was posted on the wall of the phone company office.

I listened in bewilderment as friends told me each day of some new and wonderful development. Now I was ashamed of my discouragement and bitterness. What had I done to deserve such friendship? I knew no way to thank these people—or even God. Except to renew my own resolutions to strive to be worthy.

Everybody in town seemed to be in on it. Even girls in the telephone company office in nearby Sloatsburg engineered a food sale. The proceeds of $140 went into the fund. A group from Suffern High School spent a day working at the house. A local merchant offered to outfit the kitchen and dinette with all the linoleum it needed. Merchandise to furnish the entire inside was assembled at cost. A phone company employee loaned his dump truck to the job. And my father-in-law was a tower of strength, working seven days a week for five months....

When the house was just about finished, except for some work on the inside and in the yard, I was allowed to leave the hospital for the weekend. I was driven to my new home. There, one of my buddies, Winnie Wanamaker, picked me up and carried me over the threshold.

And to think there was a dark period when my faith was at a complete low—I had lost faith in myself, my friends, and in God. Turns out, I'm one of the luckiest guys in the world to have the friends and the community to which I belong. God has been very good to me.

In everyone's life, at some time, our inner fire goes out. It is then burst into flame by an encounter with another human being. We should all be thankful for those people who rekindle the inner spirit.

ALBERT SCHWEITZER

A Friendly Move

BY NONA BRIDGES

I unpacked another box in the living room, carefully peeling away sheet after sheet of the newspaper protecting our picture frames, candleholders, and vases. For a moment I stopped and peeked out the front window, hoping to see a neighbor coming up the driveway to introduce herself. But there was no one. Only the sound of the wind. Like all the times I'd checked before.

It was late January, a month since my husband, teenage son, and I had moved into our new house, and still not a soul had come over even to say hi, let alone bring a housewarming gift. What was up with my new neighbors? I looked out the window again. The skeleton-like trees in the front yard only added to my loneliness. It was odd, at forty-three, to feel like the new kid, wondering if I was going to be accepted.

I'd been excited about the move. There was more room, a space where we could grow a garden, even a swimming pool. Most of all, we were in a real neighborhood. Where we had come from, farther out in the country, we lived next to a highway, not the kind of place where people strolled over to borrow a cup of sugar or chat after dinner. I'd so looked forward to getting to know everyone. I'd asked God to help me meet some good friends here, never imagining it would be this difficult. *Love my neighbors?* I thought. *I'd settle for just knowing their names.*

I had thought about making the effort to introduce myself. But the few times I'd seen people out in their yards it had usually been just as they were getting home or on their way out. I didn't want to impose and, well, I was busy too, rushing out the door to get to my part-time job at the college or to pick up dinner fixings at the grocery store.

I emptied a few more boxes, then decided to take a break to go to the mall. I got in the car and backed out of the driveway. Glancing behind me to look for traffic, I caught a glimpse of the house across the street. *That's odd,* I thought. There was a wooden wheelchair ramp attached to the porch. I hadn't noticed it before.

As I drove past the next-door neighbors' I saw a big blue ribbon tied to their mailbox. They must have had a baby! I felt a tingle of excitement. *I ought to get them a little gift,* I thought.

I picked up a baby blanket at the mall and had it wrapped. On the way home I stopped to deliver it, introducing myself. "That's so sweet," the young mother said, cradling her newborn. "I wish I'd been able to come over and welcome you but I've hardly had a moment...."

"I know how it is," I said. I could remember all those sleepless nights with a new baby and how exhausted I'd been. My life was a breeze compared with hers. Back home I stared out the front window at the house across the street. That wheelchair ramp. *Maybe there's something I can do to help.* Suddenly, unpacking another box of books didn't seem that important.

I whipped up a batch of cookies and took them across the street. The woman who answered the door looked tired, but when she saw the plate in my hand her face brightened. "My son broke his hip and had to move back in with us," she said. "I've barely had a chance to leave the house."

I gave her a hug, wishing I had come over sooner, but in the tightness of her embrace I felt something unexpected: friendship. That was the first of many hugs we've exchanged over the years. We've shared vegetables from our gardens, cookie recipes, sorrows, and countless joys. The best way to make friends, it turns out, is to be one.

> *In everything, do to others what*
> *you would have them do to you.*
>
> MATTHEW 7:12 (NIV)

Dee-lightful

BY LACIE GRAF HANSEN

*S*leek black trousers? Check. Teal silk blouse and patent-leather pumps? Double check. I was dressed to the nines but really didn't know why. It was my first day at my first job out of college. I'd dreamed of a career in fashion, maybe as a style editor at a magazine—something thrilling and glamorous. But from the minute I settled in at my desk and looked around, I saw how far I was from that dream: gray walls, gray carpet, gray furniture. This was no glam gig. I was a receptionist at Rockwood Retirement Community in Spokane, Washington. *What am I doing here? I'm way overdressed!*

A few months before, I'd graduated from Gonzaga University with a degree in public relations and English—full of optimism, ready to conquer the world. That summer my wonderful boyfriend, Jeremy, asked me to marry him—a romantic surprise proposal with the promise of a Caribbean honeymoon. It felt like a fairy-tale beginning to my life in the real world. He had graduated with degrees in journalism and sports management, and now had a job he loved—selling tickets for his favorite minor-league hockey team. I was certain my big break in fashion was right around the corner.

July passed. August too. Still no job. No leads. Nothing. One morning, I buffed up my résumé for the umpteenth time and prayed, *Please, God, I appreciate all the blessings You've given me, I really do. But can't You lead me to my dream job too?* By fall I'd gone from aiming for a job in fashion to scrounging the Web and classifieds for a job, any job. I was trading in pencil skirts for pajama pants, confidence for self-doubt. Why wasn't God listening? Why wasn't He giving me an opportunity to shine?

The job market stayed bleak. In late September, I came across a listing on an online job site: "Receptionist needed at Rockwood Retirement Community. Greet and assist visitors and residents, operate the telephone system, and direct callers to appropriate personnel." Okay, it wasn't a position at *Vogue*. But it was something, and I needed a paycheck, so I applied. They offered me the job.

Now here I was on my first day, wondering what I had gotten myself into. A woman's voice startled me. "Hello, who's there?" she asked.

Right away my eyes lit on her elegant red-and-black silk scarf. Christian Dior, if I wasn't mistaken. *Now that's a girl after my own heart*, I thought.

"Hi, I'm Lacie, the new receptionist," I said. "I absolutely adore your scarf. Can I help you with anything?"

"Thank you," the woman said. "I was hoping you could read this card to me. I'm partially blind. By the way, my name's Dee and I'm in apartment 712."

"I would love to! It's wonderful to meet you, Dee," I said.

I read Dee's card for her, and over the next few days we chatted more. Her life story was fascinating. She'd grown up in Minneapolis, then worked for twenty years as a flight attendant for American Airlines back when air travel was luxurious and glamorous. She married a man named Mel, a general manager for Kaiser Aluminum. His work took them to Ghana and, six years later, to Spokane when he got a job managing the 1974 World's Fair. Mel died in 2003. "I still miss him every day," she said. I told her all about Jeremy, how romantic he was, and about my hopes for a career in fashion. One day I mentioned that I'd taken fifteen years of dance classes and still found it to be a great stress reliever. "The time step is one of my favorites," I said.

"I know the time step!" Dee shouted. "My sister was a dancer on *The Burns and Allen Show* and she taught me a long time ago. Let me see if I remember how it goes..." Right there by my desk, Dee hopped and stomped through the step. Of course I had to join her. We wound up bent over, clutching our stomachs, we were laughing so hard. After that, Dee would occasionally saunter over to my desk. "Is anyone around?" she'd ask conspiratorially. "I feel like doing the time step." Word of our shared talent got around and other residents at Rockwood would ask us to perform. It became our signature showpiece.

Six months after starting at Rockwood, I still didn't have any leads for a job in fashion. But I wasn't stressing about it. I looked forward to going to work in the morning, spending time with Dee and the other residents. Sometimes, after work, I'd drop by her apartment. It was impeccably furnished with sea-blue couches, white carpet, and a dazzling crystal chandelier. She would show me old photographs, her wedding dress, keepsakes from her time in West Africa.

Dee wanted to know every detail of my upcoming wedding. "What does your dress look like, dear?" she asked.

"It's a couture-inspired off-white gown with flowers on one strap and—"

"Wait," Dee said, cutting me off. "I'll be right back."

She rummaged through her closet and emerged with an ivory beaded purse. She handed it to me along with a picture of herself holding that exact purse at President Richard Nixon's inaugural ball! "Would this match your dress?" she asked.

"Oh, Dee! It's just lovely!" It was the perfect "something old" that I needed to complete my outfit.

Dee gracefully declined her invitation to my wedding (it was a bit too far for her to travel), but as soon as

I returned from my honeymoon, she wanted to hear all about it. I described the ceremony, dancing at our reception, snorkeling with Jeremy in Curaçao and the colorful markets in Puerto Rico. Dee listened intently, then gently squeezed my hand. "Lacie, always remember to give Jeremy a kiss at night and tell him how much you love him. Don't take these times for granted. I wish I had given my dear Mel more kisses and said 'I love you' more before he passed."

Okay, Lord, I said later. *I think I get it…just because I'm not working at my dream job right now doesn't mean I'm not where I need to be.*

That August, nearly a year after I'd started at Rockwood, Jeremy got an offer for a great job in California—one we couldn't pass up. A few days before we moved, Dee sent me off with a party in her apartment. I looked around at all the residents. You know something? My self-esteem was back. And I had the job to thank. I was going to miss all my new friends, especially Dee. She'd practically become my best friend.

Dee interrupted my thoughts. "Lacie, how 'bout we do the time step real quick before dinner?"

I slid off my cheetah-print stilettos, and Dee removed her pale pink pumps. We held hands, ready to perform our duet. Yes, God had led me to a better first job than I'd ever dreamed of. A pretty glamorous one too.

This communicating of a man's self to his friend works two contrary effects; for it redoubleth joy, and cutteth griefs in half.

FRANCIS BACON

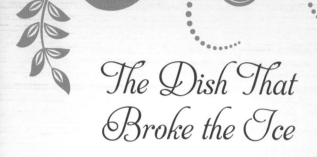

The Dish That Broke the Ice

BY SONIA LOPATUKHIN

I nudged my husband, Vladimir. "There she is," I whispered. We were walking down the hallway of our apartment complex. The "she" in question—a neighbor—was heading straight toward us. I shot her a smile. But just before our paths crossed, she abruptly turned around and hurried out of sight.

Ever since this woman and her husband had moved in the year before, I'd tried to get to know her. But I'd yet to learn her name. Each time I saw her, she'd scurry off before I could even say hello.

The man who'd lived in their apartment before had been so friendly. We invited him to barbecues, and we helped one another with errands. He became a good friend. When he moved, I assumed we'd grow just as close to our new neighbors. Our large retirement community is a friendly place. There are a lot of nods and smiles. Sometimes the gentlemen even tip their hats. For some reason she wanted no part of it.

"Is it us?" I asked Vladimir. "Have you seen her talking to any of the other neighbors?"

"Sonia, what do you care? Why do you need her to say hello?" he said.

He was right, I couldn't expect to get to know everyone. Still, it bothered me. I've always been outgoing. I would feel terrible if she thought I'd slighted or offended her. We're neighbors after all.

A few days later I was strolling through our clubhouse. I turned a corner, when suddenly she and I were face-to-face. "Hello" hardly escaped my lips before she bolted.

Why can't I get through to her? I wondered later that night. I pulled ingredients from the fridge for dinner. *Borscht*, that's what I'd make. It always made me feel better. I grated the beets, added a dash of sugar and lemon, and let the mixture simmer on the stove. My thoughts drifted back to my childhood in Russia. I could still smell Mother's *borscht*, the heady aroma of garlic and beets wafting through the house, the four of us kids clamoring for a bowl. It was perfection: rich in color, served cold with a dollop of sour cream—a spoonful was all it took to make life's worries disappear. Living under the Communist regime, we didn't have much, but Mother believed in sharing our blessings—especially the delicious food she cooked—with family, friends . . . and neighbors too. "Sonia," she'd say, "always be willing to share your last bite."

That's what I needed to do. I poured a generous helping of *borscht* into one of my prettiest bowls, walked over to our neighbors' apartment and rang the bell. The door opened a crack.

"What is it?" It was the first time I'd heard her voice.

"Hi, I'm Sonia. My husband, Vladimir, and I live right there," I said, pointing to our apartment. The door opened a little wider. "I brought you some of my homemade *borscht*."

She looked at me like I was from another planet. "I don't want to take your food," she said.

"You're not taking my food from me. I'm sharing my food with you," I said, holding out the bowl. "I don't mean to intrude; I just wanted to introduce myself."

She still looked puzzled, but she took the bowl. "Thank you," she said, then quickly shut the door.

Vladimir was eager to know what happened with our reclusive neighbor. "So, did she like the *borscht*? Did she finally say hello? Let me guess...she didn't let you in, did she?"

"Well, she took the *borscht*. Now whatever will be, will be," I told him.

A couple of days passed and we didn't see her, or her husband. *Maybe I should've minded my own business*, I thought. *I'm such a buttinsky!*

Then, on the third day, Vladimir and I came back from a walk to find my bowl outside our door, along with a beautiful bouquet of fresh flowers. There was a note too: "Thank you for the delicious *borscht*. Berta and Sam."

Berta and Sam are strangers no more. Today, we wave when we see each other and we make small talk at the community pool. I've even noticed Berta and Sam striking up conversations with other folks. We may not be best friends, but that's okay—just being friendly feels pretty great. Mother was right. It makes a difference when you share your blessings, even something as simple as a smile, or a bowl of *borscht*.

> *It is good when you obey the royal law as found in the Scriptures: "Love your neighbor as yourself."*
>
> JAMES 2:8 (NLT)

A Friend for Micah

BY STEPHANIE THOMPSON

The back door banged open. "Mommy, Mommy," called our five-year-old daughter, Micah, coming in from running errands with her father, and racing toward the kitchen. "Daddy and I saw a lost dog!" she exclaimed.

"We already have a dog," I wanted to say. As if on cue, Princess, our pug, came running.

Michael followed Micah into the kitchen. "I told Micah that dinner was waiting and if the dog didn't have a home it would still be there when we finished."

"Where was it?" I asked Michael.

"In front of the field by the corner," he said. "Just sitting there. No tags or anything."

Wayward dogs were not an uncommon sight in our rural neighborhood. In the months that we'd lived in our new house, we'd been visited by a Labrador, a Boston terrier, a miniature Schnauzer, a tiny Pomeranian, and a big white golden retriever. What we never seemed to meet was a girl

Micah's age or a mom who worked at home like I did and who might enjoy a coffee break or playdate with our kids.

I had such high hopes when we bought our house the summer before. The real estate agent said there were lots of kids in the neighborhood. There was even a girl about Micah's age right next door. I remembered growing up on a block with tons of kids and our moms exchanging recipes over the fence or sunbathing on lawn chairs while we ran through sprinklers. But in the time we'd been here, I'd hardly seen a child.

One evening I dropped by the neighbor's. The mom was nice enough and the daughter hovering behind her skirt certainly looked Micah's age, but the woman said that she and her husband worked during the day and once their daughter came home from daycare and they got dinner out of the way it was practically time for bed. "What about weekends?" I said hopefully. No, weekends wouldn't work either. They usually had a stepdaughter visiting, and their schedule was very busy....

I walked home in utter dismay. "Lord," I moaned, "I want to find a neighborhood friend for Micah and one for me too. Isn't there someone in all these houses?" As it was, I was driving twenty minutes each way for playdates in our old neighborhood.

"Mommy, can we keep the dog?" Micah asked now.

"We've got Princess," I said, dishing out supper.

"The dog probably lives in the house by the field," said Michael. "He just got out. We'll let the people know he's there."

"When can we go?"

"Soon as dinner is finished."

We ate hurriedly and piled into the car. Michael drove to the corner and slowed at the field. No dog. The sun was sinking low on the horizon, and the sky blazed with streaks of orange. I could hear a coyote howl in the woods beyond. This was not a safe place for a stray. We should have come earlier.

"There he is, getting a drink," called Micah. She pointed to a pond at the edge of the field. Michael stopped the car. I opened the door to see a small white Jack Russell lapping up the water. "Here, boy," I hollered. He looked at us quizzically and then came running. He leapt past me into the back seat and plopped right next to Micah, his front paws in her lap. We all started laughing.

"He can't be a stray," Michael said. "Not with behavior like that." We drove him to the house by the pond, but the man there shook his head. He didn't have a dog and didn't know anyone nearby who had a Jack Russell. We tried another house. Nobody there had lost a dog.

"What should we name him?" Micah said, stroking his back. I hesitated. I'd been praying for a playmate for Micah, not another dog.

Michael looked thoughtfully at Micah in the rearview mirror before pulling out of the driveway. "That black around his eye is distinctive," he finally said. "Let's call him Patch."

"For now," I added.

At home we gave Patch a bath and a bowl of food, then I took his picture and made flyers with his photo on them. That night, while Michael and Micah played with the dog, I drove four miles in each direction, taping posters on utility poles: "Have You Lost Your Dog?" I had to admit, he was pretty cute. And he was easy to have at home. Before bed I put soft blankets down on the floor of the bathroom next to our bedroom. "Here, boy," I showed him. He circled three times and lay down. The only sound we heard from there all night was soft snoring.

We didn't get one phone call about a lost dog. The next morning I put him out in the yard with Princess. Micah played with both dogs while I called all the animal shelters. No, nobody had called about a lost Jack Russell with a black patch over his eye. It was hard to believe that a dog this cute and well-behaved didn't have a home.

Over breakfast I wracked my brain about what to do. I could put an ad in the classifieds and ask more of my neighbors. If only I knew more people around. Micah practically inhaled her Cheerios so she could go back outside. But when we stood up from the table and looked out, Patch was gone.

"Mommy, where did he go?" Micah said mournfully.

"I don't know, honey. He must have gotten out." I looked at the fence we had for Princess. Evidently a Jack Russell could squeeze right out between those bars. We opened the gate and went searching in the woods behind out property. "Patch! Patch!" Micah called.

"We'll go look in the car, honey," I said. For the next hour we drove slowly around the neighborhood, checking every side street. Defeated, we came back home. I noticed a red light blinking on the answering machine. I played the message: "I saw the flyer for the lost dog...well, it must have gotten lost again because I just found it."

Micah jumped and hugged me, and I dialed the number. The woman's name was Christy. She lived only two streets away. She too had recently moved to the neighborhood and had a young son named Mason. "We'll be right over," I said. She answered the door in sweatpants and a T-shirt. "Why don't you have a cup of coffee?" she said. "We can let the kids play with the dog."

Soon Mason and Micah were tearing around the backyard, and Christy and I were talking about schools and kids and what supermarkets we liked. We glanced out at the kids throwing balls for the dog and swinging on the swing set. Micah was a year older and about a head taller than Mason, but it didn't seem to matter. She had found a friend.

"That's a pretty cute dog," Christy said.

"No one's called to claim him," I said. "I wish we could keep him ourselves, but we've got another dog at home, and this one can squeeze right out between the slats in our fence."

"Well, if you don't find his owner," Christy said, "I'd love to take him. I'm home all day, and a dog would be good company."

Perhaps I don't need to tell you any more. No one ever called about Patch despite my efforts, but that was just fine. He is very happy in his new home. Micah and I love to visit Christy and Mason, our newest best friends. They were an answer to prayer...but we needed the help of a lost dog to guide us straight to them.

Friendship is unnecessary, like philosophy, like art.... It has no survival value; rather it is one of those things that give value to survival.

C. S. LEWIS

Light in the Mist

BY HELEN BLIDE

R ain pattered down on the car as my daughter, Lisa, and I crossed the border from New York into Sussex County in New Jersey. We were on our way home from visiting my mother. A cardboard box slid back and forth on the backseat. Mom had insisted we take what looked like several meals' worth of her delicious home-cooked Polish food. "Share it with your friends," Mom suggested.

That was my immigrant mother. She never forgot the years our family had struggled when I was growing up and was always thinking of other families who might need help too.

"Hey," Lisa said, sitting up beside me. "Sussex County. Isn't this where Martha lives?"

"This is the place," I said sadly. My friend's warm, friendly face seemed to rise up before my eyes, as if she were right there with us. "But I don't know where exactly."

Losing Martha was one of the most painful things in my life. When she lived down the road, the two of us saw each other all the time. We worked out together to keep in shape, went antique shopping, talked about our children. Martha had two, a boy and a girl. When her marriage broke up, she and the children moved, but I thought I wouldn't let distance come between us. I wanted to give them all the support I could. Sometimes Martha felt like more than a friend—more like the sister I had never had.

The rain stopped, replaced by a swirling mist. I'd made this trip a hundred times. I knew where I was going. *Martha's somewhere out in that mist,* I thought as I turned on my high beams. *I just don't know where.*

On an ordinary afternoon about a year before, I'd dropped by the farm where Martha lived as a caretaker to say hi. The place was empty. A sign announced the farm had been sold. Martha was gone—no forwarding address, no good-bye. Nothing. Rumor around town said she'd moved to Sussex County, but I'd never been able to track her down.

I slowed the car as I approached a fork in the road. *God,* I asked, *watch over Martha. If she needs my help, let her get in touch!*

I prepared for a right turn and stopped. *What's that?* I thought, peering through the windshield. A bright beam of light cut through the mist in the distance. I had to follow it. I took the left fork.

"Mom, where are we going?" Lisa asked. "This isn't the way home."

"I know," I said. "But I have the strangest feeling that Martha lives right around here somewhere."

The light led us down a dead-end road. We came out of the mist. In front of us stood an old white stucco farmhouse with a red barn.

"Do you think this is it?" asked Lisa.

"Yes," I said. "I do." But how could I possibly know that? I'd never seen this farm before in my life. All those trips to visit Mom, and I'd never once wondered what was down the other fork in the road. Could it really be Martha? "You stay in the car," I told Lisa. "I'll make sure we're at the right place."

I knocked. A little girl opened the door. Blonde pigtails coming loose, a smudged face, and sad blue eyes. Her brother came up behind her. "Helen!" he said. "I'm glad you're here. I think Mom could use a friend right now."

I could see dirty dishes stacked in the sink. A pile of laundry in the corner. The house was cold. It smelled musty. *This isn't like Martha.*

"Mom's in the barn."

"Stay here with the kids," I told Lisa. I hurried to the barn, my boots sinking in the mud. Faster and faster, as if I might be too late. *Too late for what?* I pushed open the door. *Martha!* She was standing on the upper level of the barn, looking down at the piles of hay below her. Martha's back was to me. Bits of straw stuck to her green sweater and uncombed hair.

"Martha?" I said. "Is everything okay?"

She looked down at me. Martha's face was pale as a ghost, and she had dark circles under her eyes. She gave a sigh full of sadness and exhaustion but didn't seem able to speak.

I hurried up to put my arms around her. "Talk to me," I said, stroking her hair. "We've been friends a long time."

It took her a moment to get the words out. "Things got real bad, you see," she said. "I lost my job. I ran out of money. I didn't know what to do or where to turn. Then tonight..." She forced herself to get the words out. "I was going to do something drastic."

"Oh, Martha!" I said, holding her tight. "I'm so glad you didn't."

"Something stopped me," Martha said. She looked at me with her eyes full of wonder. "I asked God to send me an angel. And then an image of your face appeared in my mind."

"I'm not an angel," I said. "But it was an angel who led me to this farmhouse tonight."

I walked Martha back to the house, where Lisa and I unpacked Mom's delicious food. Martha's family would have a good dinner tonight. Then we could start on those dishes and the laundry.

Martha's life changed for the better soon afterward. She got a new job, a new house—she even fell in love. She moved again, all the way to Florida. But this time she left me an address and phone number, and promised she would call if she ever needed anything or just wanted to talk. I was ready to listen. What's more, so was God.

> *A reassuring presence, a light when times are dark, a hand reaching out, is what friendship is about.*
>
> AUTHOR UNKNOWN

Best Friends

BY B. J. TAYLOR

I didn't like Sallie at first. She breezed into our women's group, hair perfectly highlighted, a designer handbag slung over her shoulder, and introduced herself, laughing loudly. *She sure is flashy*, I thought, the complete opposite of me in my old T-shirt and jeans. I figured we'd never have anything to talk about.

Then one day I found myself sitting next to Sallie at a lunch. She seemed less lively than usual, even a little sad. "Is everything okay?" I asked tentatively.

"My dog died yesterday," she said. "I loved her for eleven years. I really miss her."

"I'm so sorry," I said. "I have a dog too. I know how you must feel." Soon we were deep in conversation about our pets, kids, spouses. "I'd love to do this again," I said.

Sallie gave me a hug. "Me too!"

Now, eleven years later, Sallie and I are best friends. She doesn't hold back—whether it's giving hugs, sending funny handmade cards, or praying for my kids—and that's what I love most about her.

Love each other with genuine affection, and take delight in honoring each other.

ROMANS 12:10 (NLT)

Gal Power

BY DORENE LEAKE

I had moved clear across the state of Washington for a fresh start following a painful divorce, and I was struggling to settle in, feeling lost and alone. More than anything, I wanted to make some friends. So I'd finally worked up the nerve to visit this church one Sunday in my new town.

Lord, let me fit in here, I prayed, hesitating in the doorway. *Surround me with friends.* I took a deep breath and walked in. I spied two women about my age sitting together. "May I sit with you?" I asked.

"Of course," the woman with silvery curls responded. "I'm Naomi, and this is Bonny." I slipped in beside them.

When the service was over, I invited the two women to lunch, and over pizza I told them a little about myself.

Naomi's husband had recently passed away. "It's not easy being alone," she agreed.

"After my husband died, like you, I just up and moved," Bonny said.

"Maybe we should start a Bible study for women like us," I suggested.

"I would really love something social," Bonny said.

We racked our brains over the following days. "What if we invite women to join us once a month for prayer, games, and refreshments?" I finally suggested.

"I'll host the first one," Naomi said. "But what should we call ourselves?"

We tossed around some ideas. Finally I said, "How about GALS—God's Amazing Love Sustains?" We laughed. Our very own acronym! Perfect. We listed the meeting in the church bulletin the next Sunday.

The following Wednesday, our first meeting, I worried that no one would show up. But one by one, the women arrived, some widowed, some divorced like me, filling Naomi's living room. We had a ball together.

Since that first meeting eleven years ago, we GALS have become like a second family: eating together, going to the movies, calling each other, sharing our lives. We take care of each other in tough times too.

God has surrounded me with friends. More than that, He has shown me, through these wonderful women, how to live up to our group's name.

> *Two are better than one, because they have a good*
> *return for their labor: if either of them falls down,*
> *one can help the other up.*

ECCLESIASTES 4:9–10 (NIV)

Reunion!

BY WALTER MILLS

I t was one of those wintry February mornings when all you want is to keep the cold out and the heat in. I sprawled out on the living room couch, reading the Charlotte paper when the telephone rang. "Hello," I said.

"This is Clay Mobley," the voice on the line answered.

I sat up straight. I hadn't spoken to Clay in about thirty years.

Back when I was nineteen and Clay was twenty, he and I and three other high school buddies had driven cross-country, from Charlotte, North Carolina, to Dayton, Washington, to work as pea pickers at a Green Giant vegetable plant. The idea was to have an adventure and earn some money to help pay for college.

We had an adventure, all right. Back in 1957 there wasn't much of an interstate highway system. We drove two-lane roads for three thousand miles in a 1951 Ford, two of us in front, three in the backseat, switching drivers every few hours. For the most part, we'd never been west of the Carolinas before.

We reached Kansas City, and the car's engine conked out. One of the guys had to call home and beg his dad to wire us money so we could repair the car and continue on. When we finally made it to the Green Giant plant after three weeks of travel, we found that our promised jobs were on hold. The pea harvest was late, so for the next ten days, till the crop arrived and the factory geared up, we had to fend for ourselves.

We had no money. "Tell you what you do," a fellow at the factory told us. "Show up at dawn tomorrow at the corner of Southeast Washington Street. That's where all the day laborers gather. If you're lucky, a farmer will drive by and offer one or all of you work, picking strawberries or baling hay."

Some days just one or two of us would find work. We always pooled whatever we made. "We've got to take care of each other," Clay said that first day, pulling his pay from his pocket when we returned from the fields. We all followed suit, adding our ten dollars apiece to the pile, then went to a local diner that night and ordered burgers, fries, Cokes—all we had earned. Until then, we had been good buddies. But now we were truly all for one, one for all.

All summer—even after landing our Green Giant jobs—we ate together, bunked together in the factory dorm, and looked out for one another. We worked from six in the evening till six in the morning on a twenty-four-hour conveyor belt line, dumping forty-nine-pound box after forty-nine-pound box of peas off a pallet into giant hoppers. I remember thinking once as I drifted off to sleep, *These are the best friends a guy could ever have*.

We had planned a long, leisurely return drive home, south to California's Yosemite Park, east through Arizona's Painted Desert and across Texas and the Deep South back to Charlotte. From there, we would head off to our junior years at college—three of us to the University of North Carolina, one to Davidson, one to Wake Forest.

It didn't work out. At least, not for me. I had been counting on making a bunch of money that summer. It was the only way I could afford to stay in college. But the blown engine we had suffered back in Kansas City had really put us in a hole. "Guys," I told the others the night before we were to leave for California, "I really can't afford it. I'm going to have to head straight back home."

They all tried to talk me out of it. "Las Vegas!" Clay said tantalizingly. "Just think of it, Walt!"

I figured we would all catch up again back home before heading off to school. But sometimes things don't work out the way you've planned. That missing money turned out to be the tipping point for me. "We don't have the money to send you back to campus," my dad said, his voice full of regret.

I ended up staying in Charlotte and getting a job at a local bank. The other four returned to college. The five of us, once so tight, drifted apart, until we communicated mainly through notes attached to our family Christmas cards. One guy moved to Alabama. Clay eventually retired from a military career and moved to Yakima, Washington, about two hundred miles from the Green Giant plant. But three of us still lived within twenty-five miles of one another.

Sometimes late in the evening, I'd sit with my wife, Phyllis, and tell her stories about that long-ago summer adventure. About how one Sunday, the five of us visited a church near the plant and met a local farm family who sold us meals each day. "Fresh blueberries for breakfast, fresh lamb chops for dinner. Delicious!" I said.

"Why don't you call your old friends?" Phyllis asked one night, after I told her more stories. But I never did.

I saw Clay once, in 1976, when we took a family vacation to the Pacific Northwest. We visited him and his family at Fort Lewis, Washington, where he was stationed in the Army. We had a wonderful stay. In his doorway as we hugged good-bye, I said, "Let's keep in touch."

"You bet," he answered. But neither of us ever followed through.

Then came Clay's phone call. "We're traveling to Pennsylvania to visit our son," he said. "What if we reroute our return flight through Charlotte? I've told my wife so many stories about our cross-country trip. I'd love to see the guys again and have her meet them too."

Truth be told, I wanted to see the guys myself. More and more, I caught myself thinking about them and our long-ago adventure. The older you get, I thought, the more you cherish old friends. The lessons I'd learned that summer—about being flexible, about trusting others, about the importance of teamwork—had stayed with me all my life. I spent my entire professional career at the bank that hired me after I returned home that summer, using those same lessons I'd learned. I'd done pretty well too. A vice president.

I tracked down the other guys, all retired now—Bob Burroughs, a former judge; John Kimbirl, a minister; and Norman Kinzie, a banker—and invited them over to my house. The minute we all sat in the living room, everyone immediately started talking. We caught each other up on our families, our lives, our children, and grandchildren.

"Remember flipping those pea boxes?" Norman asked.

"By the end of the summer, my arms were rock hard," Bob said.

"Let's see those arms now," Clay joshed. Everyone laughed. It was like the years had melted away.

It was near the end of the day when Clay had a suggestion. "Why don't we all go back in a year for a fiftieth reunion?" Everyone could stay in Yakima, he said. "I've got plenty of room."

A year later we Southerners and our wives hit the road. Or rather, Norman and his wife did. They have a big motor home, and decided to drive all the way to Yakima, Washington, retracing some of our original path and documenting it with photographs and videos. The rest of us traveled on that new-fangled transportation device, the airplane. Much easier on the back, I have to say.

Clay was ready for us. He rented a van large enough to fit us all. We toured lovely south-central Washington State, visiting Mount St. Helens, several wineries, and an apple-processing plant.

Then it was on to Dayton. "There it is!" I said, spotting the factory from the road. Soon we passed the old, familiar sign: Green Giant Road.

"Look at it," Norman said. "It looks exactly the same." Sure enough, it was the same several acres of single-story, corrugated tin and concrete buildings from fifty years ago. The plant was still in business, though under a new name now with more, larger buildings. We drove by the loading docks, where once a line of trucks had delivered a seemingly endless supply of peas.

"Remember how hot it was, even working nights?" John said.

"I don't think they'd heard of air-conditioning," Bob recalled.

We walked around the grounds for about an hour. We didn't say much. Mostly, we were lost in our own thoughts. Near the end of our tour I reached for Phyllis' hand. "Every important lesson I learned about life I got from working in this place and from living with these guys," I told her. "That summer, I learned to be a man."

We must have all been thinking the same thing, because when we climbed back into the van, we had a hard time leaving. Finally John led us in prayer, thanking God for this gift of friendship.

We're all back home now, back to our everyday lives. But with one big change. Our everyday lives include each other now, the five buddies, plus our wives. The four of us who live in North Carolina gather for dinners now, and when we do, we always phone Clay. I got a call from Norman just the other day. He wanted Clay's wife's recipe for muffins. My wife has it and has been baking them since we returned home.

Fifty years ago we traveled to Dayton, Washington, to make college money. We came back from this trip far richer, deeper friends than even that summer so many years ago, and connected in ways that still amaze us.

*As iron sharpens iron, so one person
sharpens another.*

PROVERBS 27:17 (NIV)

And Then One Day Nancy Became Beautiful

I first saw Nancy when she strode through the foyer doors of our church. Black mesh stockings stretched between white leather boots and a matching leather skirt. Her hair flamed crimson above blue eyes, and I was hypnotized as she moved toward me, for I knew Nancy to be, at twenty-two, a drug addict and a prostitute.

My protected, church-oriented life flashed neon for her. Even the dullness in her eyes could not veil the contempt she had for me. I suddenly felt I had wronged her, even though I had never seen her before. She walked past me without a word, down the aisle and directly into my husband's study.

Behind the closed door Nancy voiced her hatred for people like those straights in the foyer.

"Look, I'm a junkie. I'm a prostitute. I'm wanted by the police for hot checks. A pimp's out to get me for a bad debt." She opened her handbag and cradled a revolver in the palm of her hand. Her eyes were like flint as she spoke more to inform than to convince: "He'll never lay a hand on me." She shot a defiant look across the desk. "I'm in trouble. What are you going to do about it?"

For months my husband had been working with the local vice and narcotics squads and had seen women like Nancy. The Holy Spirit let him hear her cry for help. "Is that all?" he asked calmly.

Her eyes narrowed. She apparently had expected shock, disgust. His calm acceptance threw her momentarily.

"Well?" she snapped.

"Well?" he countered.

She whirled around and stalked across the study to the outside exit. She paused, her hand on the knob. "I can't talk tonight. I'm high. Can I see you tomorrow?" Without looking around, she added, with effort, "Please."

"Two o'clock." He gave her our home address.

That evening my husband suggested that Nancy could be serious about wanting help. I nodded, casually accepting his advice to keep cool if she should call. Aware of my naiveté, he stressed that I should not show shock, contempt or rejection, regardless of her crude revelations. Those reactions would make her feel justified in returning to drugs with me as the culprit.

The next day Nancy was on my doorstep, her liquid eyes checking me sullenly. I invited her in; she scuffed past me, flopping into a chair.

"Wanting drugs is hard to get rid of," she began. Nancy was not one for small talk. She not only hit the nail, but she sent it crashing through the wood on impact. "When I want a fix, like now, the hardest thing to do is tell somebody. I know people want to help me. I know in my heart drugs are wrong. But when I need them, I don't want help—I want a fix." Her eyes rolled back in her head, and I noticed how damp her face was becoming.

My eyes began to sting. I wanted to speak. I could not think of a thing to say. She opened her eyes and read me again. "Not this time," she said with genuine regret. She rose and left, handing a paper to me as she passed. On it was written:

Dirty Sunday
I'll more than likely sit
completely still in my easy chair
with my two bare feet
And watch the reckless rats
rush off to worship and reek
in their role of the meek
Where there they will learn how to
make one more false face to wear
in their new money-making week.

That was Nancy. She walked up and asked for my hand, whacked it good, then became offended if I did not appreciate the slap. I was irritated, but kept in mind what my husband had said.

It has always fascinated me how people like Nancy eat the scum of life, experience the ultimate in rejection and humiliation, then hold on to the myth that they have a lease on honesty. Straight people, like myself, somehow could not know or be as honest as the degraded sufferer. Our motives and actions were suspect. Our words must be scrutinized for truth. Yet she expected me to accept every word she spoke as perceptive, knowledgeable gospel. She was batting me around like a ball.

I prayed much over my attitude. A change gradually came in my thinking. As her visits continued, I began to share with her what Christ meant to me. Sometimes she laughed. Other times I knew He was speaking His love to her. It was a startling revelation the first day I realized that Nancy was worth knowing even if she never changed. When Nancy realized I felt this way she no longer had the upper hand.

Then came the afternoon when she had been unusually critical of people in general, and she made a crack about "my sort of people."

"Look, friend," I snapped, "quit walking on my feelings. You don't like people cutting you down. I don't either. Being straight doesn't mean I don't have feelings. Friends don't walk on each other, they walk with each other." I extended my hand. "Friends?"

"You think of us as friends?" she asked in half-belief.

"You're drinking my coffee, aren't you?"

Something new began for Nancy. It had begun for me earlier. It was no more than a month later that she accepted Jesus Christ and ceremonially surrendered her needle with an announcement, "I'm kicking it; cold turkey."

I accepted the news with innocent, unbridled joy. I was soon to learn the sentence she had passed upon herself. I listened to her labored breathing and heard her swallow air like a tiring swimmer. By degrees her voice deepened, slowed, and drew out into nauseated groans. The groans extended, rising in pitch, and weakening. I shall never forget her pain.

She began to attend church services three times weekly. "Boy, if my friends could see me," she hooted one evening after services. "Talking and shaking hands with all those church people." From habit, she made "church" come out sounding dirty. She flinched. "That's another habit I've got to break."

"That makes ninety," I parried without smiling. Her face exploded into a kaleidoscope of gaiety. She was beautiful.

From the first, the people of our congregation knew about Nancy. They accepted her conversion as payment in full to join the family. They had her in their homes for meals and they prayed for her as the mounting crises developed.

"I just don't get them. They know what I've been and yet they treat me like I'm one of them."

"Nancy, when will you quit enjoying self-pity?" I allowed my irritation to show. "Christ has done no greater favor for you than He has for them. He forgave us all, and not a one of us deserved it—you included. We can no more reject you than you can reject us. We're stuck with each other. You put up with us. We'll put up with you. And, thank God, Christ will put up with us all."

She looked stricken. I forced a smile and extended my hand. "Friends?"

Her blue eyes melted before me. Those were the first tears I had seen her shed. "Oh yes," she choked, grasping my hand tightly. "Thank God, yes!"

This is how we know what love is: Jesus Christ laid down his life for us. And we ought to lay down our lives for our brothers and sisters.

I JOHN 3:16 (NIV)

The Swill Gang

BY PATRICIA LORENZ

I'd closed the curtains in my family room, flipped the TV channels, and settled into my green rocker for another night alone when the phone rang. It was a woman named Sunny calling from Valdosta, Georgia.

"I just read something you wrote in *Single Parent Magazine* and I have to talk to you. I'm a single parent too and sometimes I just don't know if I can make it on my own. I thought it would help to talk to someone else who's raising children alone." We talked for an hour that night, and then Sunny called every couple of weeks.

A few months later Sunny told me she wanted to move back North, so I invited her to Milwaukee for a weekend to attend a conference for single people. She stayed for a week and bought a house while she was here. She kept calling me her best friend even though I was wallowing too deep in my own miseries to be anybody's best anything. That year was the worst of my life, and I just was not up to helping someone else solve her problems.

In fact, I needed someone who would listen to my own problems. And they were many. The man I'd dated for ten months suddenly moved to Oklahoma to start a new career. My ex-husband died of leukemia, not long after he married his girlfriend on the day our divorce was final. Our nine-year-old son, Andrew, was devastated by his father's death, but I was too angry about the divorce to know how to grieve.

That same year, my twenty-year-old daughter, Jeanne, got caught in the middle of a California earthquake, and I lived through nightmarish days until I learned she was safe. And my eighteen-year-old daughter, Julie, after graduating from high school, decided to spend the summer before college testing my sense of "loving motherhood." We hollered and picked at each other all summer. I wondered if I just couldn't get used to the idea of first Harold, then Jeanne, and now Julie leaving me. Many nights my family room felt like an empty auditorium as I sat alone with the TV set. *Lord*, I wondered, *what has happened to my family? Will this room ever seem full again?*

Then, as a favor to Sunny, after she made the move to Milwaukee with her two young daughters, I decided to gather some of my women friends to meet her. I called every woman I knew: friends from church, work, the neighborhood. Friends I met over the years through other people. Mothers of my children's friends. One from my writing club.

I was a bit nervous at first, inviting them to my house all at once, knowing that few of them knew one another. When they arrived I introduced everyone, and before long we were talking, laughing, and gabbing like old friends about our jobs, children, and lifestyles. Sunny was delighted. In fact, she said, "You people are downright interesting!"

Tina piped up, "I think we should do this every month. It can be our club. We could call it the Southeastern Wisconsin Interesting Ladies League! S-W-I-L-L."

I laughed. "SWILL! SWILL? We're going to form a club and call it *SWILL*?"

"Why not?" Sharon asked. "We can gather together, unload all the swill that creeps into our lives and get support from one another."

So we began. We decided to meet at my house every month since I had the largest family room and the fewest family members to uproot on Friday nights.

We kept it simple. SWILL would have only one rule: confidentiality. Whatever problems or heartaches discussed in that family room during our SWILL meetings would stay in that room. We would trust one another, care about one another, and help one another.

During the past three years at least twenty-five women have woven their way in and out of the SWILL meetings. Anyone can bring an interesting friend to the meetings, and if that friend likes us she can become a regular. Sometimes we've had a dozen at one time, and other months, because of hectic schedules, we've had only three or four.

As we got to know one another, we began to care more and more about one another. We became a family. I never worry about cleaning the house before a SWILL meeting because nobody's there to do a white glove inspection. And I don't worry about fancy refreshments. If one of us is having a chocolate or salty foods craving, she brings a bag of candy or pretzels to toss on the coffee table to share. But we resolved from the beginning never to get bogged down, as some clubs do, with a fancy food complex.

SWILL welcomes everyone regardless of age, race, religion, or occupation. Everyone from Carrie, a young married woman in her late twenties with four small children, struggling with the possibility of her marriage ending, to Eunice, who's been married for forty-two years and taken enough college-level classes in her retirement to be one of the most interesting people in the group.

When one member of our group, Linda, died of heart failure at age thirty-nine after meeting with us only a short time, we mourned together. Later we discussed ways to solve the medical insurance problems that often face single, overstressed parents, like Linda, who had worked as many as three jobs to make ends meet.

When Jody's teenage son, Daniel, died in a car accident, we held one another and cried with Jody at the funeral.

When Gail, whose children were starting college, went back to school to study nursing, we spent hours talking her into staying in school when she wanted to quit. One of our members, a counselor, helped Gail through some test anxiety problems one night. Gail graduated in May, and we all took a bow.

When Barb's son came home from Desert Storm and moved back into her and her husband's "empty nest," and then a few months later her daughter moved back home with her husband and new baby, we listened to the ups and downs of Barb's five-adults-in-one-house, three-generation family. We gave her lots of advice, including the fact that it was okay for her to go back to work full-time.

Carol, whose solid marriage rubs off on all of us, points out that even a happy marriage isn't perfect all the time, but that a sense of humor can get you through most of the swill that marriages can dish out.

Sunny benefited tremendously from SWILL. She became more independent, found a wonderful job in the Milwaukee school system, made lots of new friends at work, in her neighborhood, and in her church, and moved on to start her own support network.

What did SWILL do for me, the one who was simply trying to find a few friends for Sunny? I think I'm the one who benefited most. These women—single, separated, divorced, married, from all walks of life—opened their hearts and their lives to me, month after month. They listened to me, laughed with me, and helped me through the rough times of being a single parent. Now that I have three children in college at once and a twelve-year-old at home, they help me even more through the struggles by offering financial advice as well as emotional help. I've learned to talk about my fears and my failures, and to admit that I'm scared at times and that it's okay to have conflicts with the ones you love.

I've also learned how important it is to get out of the house and get plenty of exercise. Gail and I started roller skating two or three times a week on the bike path near Lake Michigan. And Betsy (another SWILL member) and I speed-walk every Saturday morning for an hour. I lost thirty-five pounds and have never felt better physically in my life.

One thing's for sure—the years following my worst year ever were better by far because of the interesting and loving women friends I made through SWILL. And, well, I'm just wondering if we shouldn't change our name to SWELL. Because we are. A swell bunch of women who, during the past few years, have become a family to one another, a nonjudgmental support system that's always there on the first Friday of each month.

Once again, the good Lord has filled my family room with "family." A new family of friends. It's amazing how much love I feel now that I've learned to open up my life to these friends and to nourish that friendship on a regular basis.

> *Friendship is born at that moment when one person says to another: "What! You too? I thought I was the only one."*
>
> C. S. LEWIS

A Friend Like Patsy

BY PENNEY SCHWAB

M y friend, Patsy, and I usually sat on either end of the pew, sandwiching our wiggly preschoolers between us. Today we sat side by side. It was my last Sunday in the church we both loved. At dawn tomorrow our family was moving to a farm near Copeland, Kansas.

I'd miss the church and our friendly Texas town. I'd miss living just down the road from my husband's parents. But most of all, I'd miss my friends. Especially Patsy.

Patsy shared all the bits and pieces of my life. Every Thursday evening she sat at my kitchen table and fed strained carrots to six-month-old Rebecca while I taught her oldest sons to play my battered upright piano. We shared recipes: my fifty hamburger dinners (we raised beef) and Patsy's zillion ways with zucchini (she loved to garden).

We helped with each other's moneymaking projects. Patsy's "earthworm experiment" went great until we had to sort five hundred creepy night crawlers from tubs of manure. My cattle-checking venture was fun—until we saw a diamondback rattler on a day we'd worn shorts and sandals to hunt for calves.

We team-taught the junior-high Sunday school class, provided oatmeal cookies for the Cherub Choir, and took our kids for picnics when our husbands worked late.

What would I do without Patsy?

She read my mind. "You'll make new friends right away," she whispered, squeezing my hand.

"Not like you," I whispered back, choking down the lump in my throat. I already knew there wouldn't be any friends like Patsy in Kansas. Everyone said so.

The elderly couple from whom we'd be renting the farmland said so. "My dear," they told me, "prepare to be very lonely. There simply aren't any young people around here."

My mother said so: "Small towns aren't always friendly to strangers."

Don's mother said so: "It will be hard to meet anyone with you living eight miles out in the country. It's a good thing the children have each other for playmates."

The children had each other. Don had the farm. But what about me?

Patsy nudged my arm, and we stood for the closing hymn, "What a Friend We Have in Jesus." I knew the Lord was my Friend...and the most wonderful Friend anyone could have. But I needed earthly friends too.

Dear Lord, I prayed as the pastor gave the benediction, *please give me a friend just like Patsy.*

We set out for Kansas at seven o'clock on a chilly Monday morning in February. I drove our old white station wagon crammed with three children and a week's worth of clothing. A family friend loaded our furniture and appliances onto his truck, and also carried our German shepherds, Andi and Robert. Don's blue pickup brought up the rear. The back was piled with roped-down boxes of pots and pans, books, and the baby bed. On the seat beside him Don had a basket of green-and-yellow tissue-paper flowers—the last project Patsy and I had done together.

We were a modern-day wagon train. I was certain we were heading into hostile territory.

We arrived at the farm too late to begin unloading, so we spent the night at a motel in a neighboring town. The next day, we got the kind of Kansas welcome I'd dreaded. While we ate breakfast, light snowflakes turned into a snowstorm by noon and into a raging blizzard by early evening. Andi and Robert, disoriented by the snow, ran away.

I'd never felt so alone. I sank down on a soggy carton, one that was dripping melting snow all over the kitchen, and started to cry.

Then the telephone rang. I was so startled I let it ring again and again. Who could it be? I'd thought the line was still unconnected, and no one even knew we were here.

Finally I picked up the receiver. "Hello?"

"Welcome!" a friendly voice said. "I'm Audrey Button. I live in the yellow house two miles straight east. This weather is getting nasty, so I thought you might want to know how to use the phone, because it's an eight-party line, and who to call if you need help."

She gave me a list of numbers, then we visited for several minutes. *Maybe this is the friend I prayed for*, I thought, *the one just like Patsy*. But no. Mrs. Button's girls were grown and gone, and she and her husband were semiretired. She was nice, but not at all like Patsy.

After two days of snow, the weather warmed up. I discovered there was something worse than being snowbound: We were now marooned by mud. Our two and a half miles of dirt road (heavy clay soil at that) dissolved into an impassable quagmire.

That's why we were surprised when, about nine o'clock one night, there was a knock at the door. "We're Howard and Ruth Stude," a pleasant, middle-aged couple introduced themselves. "We're your third-to-nearest neighbors." They apologized for coming so late and explained they'd been afraid to try our roads before they froze semisolid.

"We hope you'll come to our church," Ruth invited.

"We'll see," I hedged. The church she described sounded nice, but it couldn't possibly be like the one I'd left.

We went that Sunday anyway. The people were friendly, and the building was lovely. There were two little girls Patrick's age and twins who were nearly four, like Michael. But no babies, and no one who looked like a replacement for Patsy.

That week I went to Copeland's one small grocery store. The aisles were very narrow, and Rebecca amused herself by grabbing things from one side while I was on the other—a box of oatmeal while I was searching for rice, a can of beans while I stocked up on corn. And she did it all from the seat of the shopping cart.

I was afraid I'd be banned. But Annie and Edith, the proprietors, just laughed. "We've been thinking of building a bigger grocery," Edith said. "If your baby is going to be a regular customer, we'll do it for sure."

Annie made a sign about my dogs: Lost south of Copeland, two silver German shepherds. She posted it in the front window. (A week later the dogs were home, safe and sound.)

On my next visit to town I noticed a tiny building of corrugated tin right underneath the water tower. *Copeland Public Library*, a white sign read. *Hours 2-5 Tuesday and Thursday*.

It was 2:30 PM on Thursday, so I went in. The librarian was a frail woman with sparkling blue eyes and hair as gray as the building.

"I'm new here," I told her. "Can I apply for a library card without having someone cosign it?" (My old library required two character references.)

"My dear, choose as many books as you like!" the librarian said. "Just sign your name on each card."

I chose three and took them to the desk. She stamped them, then indicated a chair next to her. "I'm Mrs. Ewing," she said. "If you have time, tell me about yourself."

We had a wonderful visit—the first of many. But much as I liked her, she wasn't the right age to be another Patsy.

Several weeks passed. My closest neighbor, Neva Patterson, held a get-acquainted coffee for Don and me. It was loads of fun, and I met many interesting people. But not one could replace Patsy.

When Patsy called to see how I was adjusting, I told her so. "I've met lots of lovely people," I said, "but they're all too old, or they don't have kids the ages of mine, or we aren't interested in the same things."

"So what?" Patsy replied. "You and I aren't the same age, and we didn't have much in common when we first met. You liked sports, I liked sewing. You read mysteries, I preferred romances. You liked comedies, I went for long, sad movies."

Funny, I'd forgotten all that. I'd forgotten that my friendship with Patsy had developed slowly and deepened over a period of years.

"You'll never have another friend like me," Patsy continued, "because I'm one of a kind. God only makes originals, you know. No carbon copies."

No carbon copies!

In my search for a friend "just like Patsy," I'd overlooked the many "originals" God had sent my way. People like Mrs. Ewing, the store ladies, my wonderful neighbors. Friendship, I realized as Patsy and I said good-bye, wasn't a matter of age or family or common interests. It was sharing, and caring, and growing together. And it rarely came instantly.

God had been answering my prayers for a friend since our first day in Copeland. He'd brought a whole community of people into my life. In time, I'd have friendships just as beautiful and deep as the one Patsy and I shared.

Nature has no love for solitude, and always leans, as it were, on some support; and the sweetest support is found in the most intimate friendship.

CICERO

The Old Bureau

BY HAZEL F. ZIEMAN

I would never have believed an old bureau could have caused such bitterness between Barbara and me. Next-door neighbors for six years, we were close friends, one or the other always on hand if needed.

But then came the sale. Distant cousins of mine were moving out of state. They had to get rid of much of their furniture.

"She's letting several of her lovely pieces go," I told Barbara. "One of them is a bureau of solid walnut, over a hundred years old. You must go with me to the sale."

"Always trying to get me interested in antiques." Barbara laughed. "All right, I'll go."

"And be prepared to buy something this time," I urged her.

My grandmother had told me how great-great Uncle Ned had built the bureau, had carved the oak-leaf handles himself, had taken it across the country in a covered wagon. I'd admired the bureau many times, not dreaming I'd have the chance to own it.

At my cousin's suggestion, we went over very early the day of the sale, so we could choose any of the things we wished. My cousin was on the phone when we got there, but her husband began to show us around. I was looking at some old pieces of silver, waiting to tell my cousin I'd take the bureau, when Barbara walked up and said, "Well, I did it. I bought something."

"Good! Show me what you got," I said. She took me over and pointed to the bureau. "Not my bureau!" I must have shouted, for Barbara backed off, looking shocked and hurt.

"Your bureau! I thought that's what you wanted me to buy," she said.

I must have gone temporarily insane. I said some awful things to Barbara: How she knew I wanted that bureau more than anything in the world. How I thought she was my friend. How I hated her for this. Barbara ran out of the house. I never did find out how she got home.

I felt sick inside. Several times in the next few days, I started to go over to apologize. When I finally did get up my nerve, Barbara saw me coming and ran from her yard into the house. I didn't know what to do, so I went back home. Weeks passed without our talking with each other.

One day, we unexpectedly came face to face in the super-market. Both of us stammered "Hello," but that was all. Gradually the whole thing began to look pretty ridiculous to me. I'd got us into this mess and I'd get us out.

So I went over and rang Barbara's doorbell. "This whole thing is silly," I said.

"I've known that for a long time," she answered. But her voice was icy, and she didn't smile.

I choked up and turned away. How could she make it so hard for me?

The next month, at a PTA meeting, Barbara and I were both assigned to the planning committee for our annual spring festival. I thanked God for another chance. Maybe Barbara would have changed her mind by now and be willing to meet me halfway. But when the committee met, she didn't show up. "Isn't Barbara coming?" I asked the chairman.

"Said she couldn't possibly serve. Personal reasons."

Well! I thought. *This is certainly a slap in the face!*

A strange ugliness settled inside me. It squeezed my throat muscles, slithered into my head, until the pressure gave me a headache.

When my cousin had phoned to say Barbara didn't want the bureau and when would I like to pick it up, I had told her to take one of the other offers she had on it, that I never wanted to see it again. And now I hated it more than ever.

One day I was reading my Bible for a few minutes after the children left for school. I'd got into the book of Ephesians and was starting the fourth chapter. A couple of lines pricked at me.

"Accept life with humility and patience, making allowances for one another" (Ephesians 4:2, PHILLIPS).

I read that passage over and over. "Making allowances... because you love one another." Hadn't I tried to love Barbara with Christian love? Then I put the Bible down and kneeled beside my bed in desperation.

"God," I prayed, "this is such a little thing, but it's got so terribly big inside of me. All I can feel for Barbara is resentment. I've tried to love her, but it just doesn't seem to work. I know You have enough love. If I could just borrow from You for a while, I'm sure the feeling will come to me."

A great sense of relief filled me. I moved happily through my household routine and felt a joyous anticipation for my husband and children's homecoming and our family dinner, for the countless little things of the next few days.

But God wasn't through with me. A couple of days later, as I was reading Ephesians, I came across these words: "If you are angry, be sure that it is not out of wounded pride or bad temper" (Ephesians 4:26, PHILLIPS).

No wonder I hadn't been able to feel Christian love. All this time I'd been blaming Barbara for refusing to do her part. It began to be clear that God expected something more of me. If His love was going to show through me, it needed some sort of action on my part.

I was going to have to demonstrate my feelings. Several times that week, I called "hello" to Barbara across the backyard fence. By the end of the week, she answered my greeting.

Open house at school was coming up the next Tuesday, so I went over to her house that morning.

"Barbara, I'm going down to open house tonight. Won't you ride with me?"

She hesitated, giving me a long, puzzled look. Silently I prayed, *God bless you, Barbara*, and I tried to beam a feeling of love toward her. Out loud I said, "I'd really like to have you."

I'm sure she felt something, for she smiled suddenly. "All right," she said.

Every time I was with Barbara, I beamed love toward her. It wasn't long until our old relationship had returned.

I know those verses from Ephesians by heart now. They taught me that what I can do is pretty limited. But what God can do through me, if I let Him, is something else again.

> *Love prospers when a fault is forgiven, but dwelling on it separates close friends.*
>
> PROVERBS 17:9 (NLT)

My Unknown Friends

BY RUTH BRUNS

I t was the last morning of the four-day conference. Someone among us had asked for our prayers. We sat around the room, heads bowed, and prayed for an "unknown friend."

Through the corner of my eye, I watched my neighbor, sitting with closed eyes and rapt face. Four days before, on first seeing her modest dress, her quiet face, I had winced, thinking, *This one's a wet blanket*.

Now I watched her with affection, for I had come to know her as a warm, delightful person. All around the room I could see others whom I had thought dull or antagonistic or shallow, until I came to know them. How well the phrase "unknown friend" described these people. I had thought I was meeting strangers, but I was really meeting friends, waiting to be known.

Twelve hours later, I stood in line to board a plane home. The young man in front of me stepped back and stumbled against my bag, knocking it over. He muttered something under his breath. A sharp retort sprang to my mind, for I didn't like his long-haired looks anyway. Then the thought came: *Maybe this is another unknown friend*.

Swallowing hard, I smiled at him and said I was sorry the bag was in his way. "It's a typewriter," I apologized. "I couldn't check it through with my luggage."

The young man looked surprised. Then he smiled, and from behind the long hair and bushy beard, a cheerful, friendly boy looked out at me. "It must be heavy," he said. And he carried the typewriter on the plane and tucked it under my seat.

All the way home, I wondered what the world would be like if each of us remembered to show to those who cross our paths the same courtesy and tolerance we show to friends. It shouldn't be hard to do. We have only to see, behind each new face, not a stranger, but an unknown friend.

The glory of friendship is not the outstretched hand, not the kindly smile, nor the joy of companionship; it is the spiritual inspiration that comes to one when you discover that someone else believes in you and is willing to trust you with a friendship.

RALPH WALDO EMERSON

My Friend the Stranger

BY MEREDITH SUTTON

I t was one of those unforgettable experiences that transcend time, language, customs. President Nixon was en route back to America after his trip around the world following the first moon landing in 1969. I was the pilot of one of the president's backup planes.

We stopped in Bucharest, Romania, for a short visit. It was late afternoon as I stood on the steps of our hotel, which overlooked a large city square. I watched the flow of people going home from work.

Most were dressed in clothing resembling pre-World War II American styles, except that many of them wore fur hats. Mingling with this city throng were men and women whose garb labeled them as being from some of the outlying villages. A few appeared to be sheepherders, and I guessed some of the more roughly dressed men to be woodcutters or miners.

What a different world this was from the Asian one we had left only a few hours before. I scanned the faces close to me and listened in vain for any English. Suddenly I wanted to talk to someone. But I didn't know any Romanian or even Italian, which might have helped.

After a few moments, I heard a melody long familiar to me, floating clearly and unmistakably above the confusion of sounds. Someone was whistling an old English hymn we had sung in our church for years. Somewhere in that crowd there was a Christian. Impulsively I plunged down into the milling throng and headed in the direction of the whistler.

Oh, I thought, *if only he will keep it up through another verse!*

I was pushing against the flow of the crowd. Still, I heard the thin, high sound of the whistled tune. It seemed to be moving away.

Then, there he was—a man dressed in the style of a factory worker. He wore a plaid flannel shirt, a heavy coarse jacket, and a Russian-style *karakul* hat. Under his arm was a big black lunch box just like the one I had carried on my first job.

I tapped him on the arm, talking excitedly at the same time. He stopped whistling, stiffened, and replied in Romanian. We couldn't speak to each other after all. Feeling uncertain, I stood smiling and I pointed at him, then at myself, and then above. As I did this, I took a deep breath and began to whistle the chorus of the same hymn: "The Great Redeemer Now Is Nigh."

A broad smile lit up his face, and he grasped my shoulders, pounded me on the back, and kissed me on both cheeks in the manner of the Europeans. Without wasting another moment, he began to pull me along with him. He kept smiling and gestured that we would eat together.

Turning into a side street, we suddenly left the din of the boulevard behind. It seemed as though we lost a century in time. Some houses had high thatched roofs, while others had Roman arches and carved porticos with galleries and wrought iron gates.

It was one of those old stone houses that we finally entered. I stood watching as his family hurried to greet him. He began to whistle the hymn that had brought us together, and they all broke into excited conversation. His wife shyly shook hands with me and laid a place for me at their table.

My new friend bowed his head to say grace and when he had finished, he nodded to me and I gave thanks too—thanks especially that there is One Who can bring all men together, even though they are separated by language, customs, geography, and birth. Thanks for Jesus Christ.

There is neither Jew nor Gentile, neither slave nor free . . . for you are all one in Christ Jesus.

GALATIANS 3:28 (NIV)

The Day I Became a Neighbor

BY MARION L. MCCLINTOCK

Some years ago my husband, Earl, and our two young children moved to California from a large Eastern city.

I resented the move; it was a wrench to leave my family and friends. Worse, we'd put all our furniture in storage and had rented a small, furnished house in a nondescript neighborhood near Earl's new job.

The furniture was a motley array of unmatched pieces, nicked and scratched by former users, and would not respond to my vigorous cleaning and polishing.

But my greatest desolation was my utter loneliness. I would sit for hours and cry.

Earl suggested I make friends with the neighborhood women. But I was so homesick that I shrank within a wall around myself.

When Earl spoke of inviting people from his office for a visit, I said no. I was ashamed for anyone to see our home.

Another thing about the house that bothered me was the constant presence of flies and other bugs. I sprayed and swatted them all over the house. Whenever I went out or came in the house, I always stopped at the door and waved away any flying creatures that might be lurking nearby.

At the end of our street was a house with a porch where an elderly man sat for most of the day. I guessed that he was ill.

One day my doorbell rang. I hastily removed my apron and ran into the bedroom to smooth my hair and powder my nose. "It's probably just a door-to-door salesman," I told myself, but I was determined to present myself as a proper "lady of the house."

The forlorn-looking woman on my steps was not selling anything. Her hair was unkempt, her clothes hung loosely on her, and her eyes were red and swollen from weeping. She looked familiar.

"Come in," I said. "Please sit down." While she was seating herself, I quickly whisked a small rug over the worn place in the carpet.

"I'm sorry to bother you," she said, twisting a damp ball of handkerchief in her lap. "I wouldn't have the nerve to ask you this, but I know you were always so friendly to my father."

I got up and turned off the radio so she couldn't see my startled look.

"Your father?" I managed to say.

"Oh, I'm sorry," she replied. "I guess you didn't know. He passed away last night." She fought back tears.

"My father," she went on, "was lonely in his last days. He did not know many people here. We came here from a Midwestern town where we knew everyone, and they knew us. You'll never know how much it meant to him to have you wave when you went in and out of your door. But he couldn't wave back. His arms were paralyzed."

Tears of shame rolled down my cheeks at the undeserved tribute. Then she asked if she could borrow a black coat she had seen me wearing. She wanted to wear it to her father's funeral. I eagerly got it for her.

When she left, I knew that I had reached a turning point. My self-pity and self-centeredness were the real causes of my loneliness. I had prayed for a way out of my loneliness, and God had shown me the way. I knew now that I had to make the first move, the first overture to friendship.

That night I greeted Earl at the door with a smile and even overlooked the dirt the children tracked in behind him.

The next day I joined the other neighbors in providing home-cooked meals for the bereaved family. A few days later, when I learned a young housewife on our block was expecting her first baby, I gave a shower for her at our home and invited all the other women on the block. No one seemed to notice the old furniture—nor did I anymore.

Months later we moved to another part of California. But this time there was no loneliness, no depressing period of adjustment. For I remembered the lesson I had learned from the old gentleman who mistook my angry arm waving for an act of friendliness.

This time it was no mistake—my greetings really were friendly. And I again found good neighbors by being one.

> *Love begins at home, and it is not how much we do ... but how much love we put in that action.*
>
> MOTHER TERESA

Call to a Stranger

BY LOIS SOLIE JOHNSON

O ut of Control Car Kills Child and Injures Babysitter."

How awful! I thought as I read the front-page headline. The picture showed only a part of the car. The rest was inside the living room. A car had careened across the street, jumped the lane divider and crashed into the living room of a house, killing a baby and seriously injuring the child's babysitter.

The horror of the situation gripped me. In one fleeting moment, a mother had lost her baby, and a young girl's life might have been irrevocably altered. My heart went out to these people.

Then some new thoughts struck me. What about the woman who was driving the car? How would people feel toward her? How much sympathy and understanding would she receive? How would I feel if this had happened to me?

An urge grew within me to do something about her. I had felt a similar urge in other situations, but it had been so easy to hide behind my pots and pans, church activities, lack of a second car, any number of other things.

I clipped the article from the paper and put it in a drawer where it stayed for several days as one insidious whisper after another came to me: "You don't even know this woman." "You don't have any idea what kind of a person she is." "She might resent you." "It's really none of your business."

But my heart ached for her and I couldn't get her off my mind. "Bear ye one another's burdens" (Galatians 6:2, KJV). How often I'd heard those words. I'd even glibly spoken them at times. But putting them into practice was something else.

Praying for guidance, I wrote to Marge—that was her name—expressing my deep concern for her. I told her that God could bring good out of any situation, no matter how tragic, and that in Jesus Christ she could find the answer to her needs, just as I had. Then I waited and kept on praying.

Several days later Marge telephoned. After we had talked a long time, she readily consented when I asked if I might visit her.

As Marge's husband opened the door, I was met by a fog of depression so intense it almost overwhelmed me. Getting up from her chair slowly, as though every movement were too great an effort, Marge led the way to the dining room and offered me coffee.

"Why would you, a complete stranger, care anything about me?" she asked. "Nobody has ever done anything like this before."

The coffee grew cold as, with tear-filled eyes, she poured out her story. Two years before, the family had moved from a distant state, leaving relatives behind. They had not attended church for years, and she had no friends. Though financially strapped, they had just begun to get ahead.

"We were coming home from my brother-in-law's house," Marge explained. "My husband had had too much to drink so I wouldn't let him drive."

"And you?" I asked.

"I only had a few drinks."

Her face mirrored utter dejection when I asked about insurance. "I put the premium notice on a shelf and forgot about it."

An added blow came when her mother, whom she desperately needed, was unable to come because of illness. A crushing burden of guilt and despair had all but drowned Marge emotionally.

I had prayed before I went that I would be filled with love for this person whom I had never met. As I watched her across the table, I knew that God had already answered that prayer. I did love her. And I longed to be able to lift the heavy load from her heart. I couldn't, of course; but as I began to tell her of the One Who could, I knew He was there.

It was thrilling to see Marge open up to God's forgiveness and love. Because her sense of guilt was so profound, this did not happen suddenly. "How can I know that I can be forgiven?" she pleaded.

"Would you like to come with me tomorrow afternoon?" I asked just before leaving. "A few of us meet each week to share problems and to help each other grow spiritually." Her reply indicated genuine interest, so the following day I picked her up.

Being with new people usually made her nervous, she had told me, but this time she must have felt at home. Week after week she continued to come. Unable to go back to work or do her housework because of injuries resulting from the accident, she spent hours each day reading the Bible and Christian books and periodicals.

Though she participated freely in our sharing time, she did not have the courage to pray out loud. So we were startled one afternoon, as our heads were bowed in prayer, to hear her voice. "Dear Lord," she began, "You know how hard it is for me to pray out loud, so I took the easy way out and wrote this down." Brokenly, she continued. We wept too as she thanked God for her new friends and for all He had done for her since she had given her life to Him.

When surgery was necessary to correct improper healing of Marge's injuries, her new friends took meals to her home. Then when the shock of a six-month jail term came (because of the accident), Marge's family was surrounded with love and prayerful concern. Few visitors were permitted, but the number of letters Marge received prompted one inmate to say, "It must be wonderful to have people care about you."

Many problems remain, even since Marge's release from jail. Yet her faith remains strong. She wrote not long ago, "Trusting in the Lord makes everything so much easier. There is this wonderful sense of peace. It's not through my power but God's that I'm holding up."

When I think of all that has happened since the day I first saw those headlines, I pray with all my heart that whenever God gives me a nudge, I'll never fail to move.

As God's chosen people, holy and dearly loved, clothe yourselves with compassion, kindness, humility, gentleness and patience.

COLOSSIANS 3:12 (NIV)

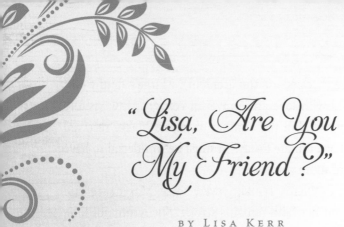

"Lisa, Are You My Friend?"

BY LISA KERR

I was fourteen and a pain in the neck, to be honest. I mean, I'd just run away from home; the best friend I'd ever had betrayed me in a way I never thought possible; my parents thought I was insane; and the only friends I had hung around me because, at the time, being a trouble-maker's friend meant you were "cool."

The people I hung around ate up the stories I fed them of excitement and mischief. I suppose they respected me in some twisted way for having guts or something like that. But when I just wanted to be held or comforted, none of those "friends" were around.

The only person I felt deeply about, a boyfriend, I was no longer allowed to see. At first I prayed to God, "Please, please send me someone or something I can love again." Then after a while I stopped caring altogether. I had finally convinced myself, and everyone around me, that I had no need for anyone but myself.

I suppose that is when I became a real strain to deal with. And when my parents insisted that I had to spend the first two weeks of my summer working at a day camp for developmentally disabled kids, I acted mad. I wasn't really mad, just scared. Actually, I liked kids a lot. I told myself it could be worse. However, I didn't feel that way that very first day.

The volunteers and staff were required to ride the buses to keep order on the way to camp. I stepped up on the bus, smiled at the woman who was driving and reluctantly headed toward a seat. There were about five kids on the bus already. I tried not to look at any of them too long, smiling weakly and blindly at each as I passed. They grinned shyly back.

"Sit across from me!"

I turned my head to see a heavyset young girl sitting in a seat, holding a tiny blond boy. "Right here," she said, slapping the seat across the aisle while balancing the small child dangerously on her other knee.

Almost afraid to say no, I sat where she told me, and before I knew it she was unloading her burden on me. "You hold Robby now," she said. "You work here, not me."

Looking down, I found myself staring into the large, vacant blue eyes of the little boy now in my lap. His mouth was open and wet, and his head bobbed up and down rhythmically as the bus bumped along the road.

"He can't talk," came the voice from across the aisle.

The heavyset girl's eyes were still fixed on me. I was nervous but I tried to be kind.

"Oh," I said, "well, what's your name?"

"Karen," she beamed proudly. "I always hold Robby, but now you can. What's your name, girl?"

"Lisa."

"How old are you, girl?"

"Fourteen."

"Ha!" she laughed loudly, pointing a kindly teasing finger at me. "You a baby. I'm seventeen!"

Seventeen! She acted like a three-year-old.

"Well, how old is Robby?"

"Six."

I was shocked. Robby was about the size of a two-year-old and he couldn't talk. He was a beautiful child, but he just kept babbling and rolling out sounds. His expression was blank; still, as the bus bounced and jolted along, he clung to me as if he knew I was there to protect him.

"You just wait till them crazies get on the bus," Karen was telling me. "Some of them really crazy." She tapped her temple with one finger, then moved it around in a circle.

I laughed. "Everybody's a little bit crazy."

"*Hmph*!" she said, throwing back her head. "You wait."

Robby was now standing and leaning toward the window. I slid over so he was right next to it. With his small hand he began spastically banging on the glass and calling, "Wawa." He was smiling. I looked out the window. We were crossing a bridge.

"Water," I said out loud. "I thought he couldn't talk," I told Karen.

She shrugged uncaringly. "He can a little."

"Robby, say Lisa," I said with slow deliberation. "Lisa." I pointed a finger to my chest. "Li-sa," I repeated.

For a moment he looked at me blankly, as if I were an idiot. Then he stretched forth a hand and put it on my chest. "Nana," he said.

I nodded happily. "Yeah. Lisa."

"Nana," he repeated, nodding his doll-baby head.

Karen broke into a childish round of laughter. "He called you Momma!"

"Nana," I corrected her, rolling my eyes.

As the bus began to fill up I grew apprehensive. Strange faces loomed at me from almost every seat. A few other volunteers and staff boarded and smiled, but none I took a particular interest in. Mostly there were children. Some of them asked me over and over again who I was.

Others just swung shy faces my way from the front of the bus. I felt like an exhibit. Even the staff seemed to be checking me out.

I didn't care what any of them thought. I was only doing this because I had to, not to please any of them or to hang around these kids for two weeks. Did they really think I cared?

A pair of green eyes winked at me from the seat in front of mine. I stared back. All I could see was a round shaved head and the squinty eyes that kept watching me.

"Hi," I said, to do something to break the discomforting stare.

A round, cherub-like face with buck teeth and no chin popped up quickly and grinned at me.

"Hi," said the little man. "I'm Brad. I'm gonna marry you."

"What?"

"I'm gonna marry you," he repeated, grinning slyly. "You gonna be my wife, you gonna be my wife," he began saying in a singsong chant.

I rolled my eyes again. *Oh, God, why have You put me here? All these people are going to do is make me crazier. Why am I here?*

Brad followed me around the rest of the morning until the campers were divided into groups by age. I breathed a sigh of relief when I found I'd be working with kids from eight to twelve years old; Brad was twenty-six. I thanked God.

By the end of that day, though, I'd acquired more "followers." There was Charles, the freckle-faced kiss-o-holic who grabbed me and planted one on me every chance he got, and Daniel, a skinny, grinning little boy who sweetly slipped his hand around my waist and asked me to be his "best girl."

And there was Jeni.

Jeni was a chubby, thirteen-year-old girl with short, curly brown hair, a pug nose, and large, liquid-chocolate eyes. She followed me around, continuously asking questions:

"Lisa, what did you have for breakfast?"

"Cereal, Jeni."

"Lisa, what's your middle name?"

"Katherine....Now hang on, Jeni, I'm doing something."

"Okay...Lisa, what are you doing?"

"Jeni!"

Her questions drove me out of my mind. All the kids did. I didn't want them to follow me or hug me or hold my hand. How could they be so presumptuous to think I wanted their attention? How could they expect me to care about them? I didn't even know them. I didn't want to. I was afraid to.

That night, I told my mom I wasn't going back. Of course, she told me I had no choice. So I went to my room and pouted, and once again told God, "This isn't doing me any good, God. I need something more. I need a friend. These kids depend on me to take care of them, but, God, I need someone to take care of me. Please help me."

No divine revelation came to me that night, so the next day I returned to camp, praying that the time might at least pass quickly.

On the bus, Robby was piled on my lap again, Brad sat beside me, and Charles was waiting for me as I stepped off the bus. He placed a sloppy kiss on my mouth.

"Thanks a lot," I told him sarcastically.

He in turn flew into a hideous laughing fit and dashed madly across the playground to stalk another victim.

As soon as arts and crafts started, Jeni spotted me. I took a frustrated breath as she came and stood behind me.

"Hi, Lisa."

"Hi, Jeni," I tossed back at her half-heartedly.

"I missed you," she said.

I stopped what I was doing. Slowly I turned to Jeni, feeling an odd, almost warm sensation run through me. I faced her then. She was gazing at me with a tender, honest expression, waiting patiently for my answer.

"I—uh—thanks," I finally managed to spit out. I smiled at her with an unwonted feeling of gratitude. For what, I wasn't sure.

"Jeni," one of the staff members called, "come start your picture." Without another word to me, Jeni started off.

Before I even thought about what I was risking, I called, "Jeni, do you want to be my swimming buddy today?"

She turned, grinned a pleased, beautiful grin, nodded, and then kept walking.

Suddenly, Charles's kisses weren't so bad, and Brad's proposals were actually kind of flattering. Every day on the bus, Robby would reach for me and call "Nana." I would look at the little doll of a boy and wonder, *Why do you want me? What good am I? And why do I want you to need me?* All of a sudden I found myself looking at those children in a new, glorious light.

I had learned something very special about those children. They didn't have any standards that they expected me to live up to. Whether or not I was kind to them, they would always be kind to me. Their love was pure and innocent and unconditional. I had been so wrong to think them foolish for being so open with me before they even knew me. That was their gift, their wonderful gift from God. I was amazed and touched by the love they gave me. They would have loved me whether or not I ever learned to love them back. Perhaps their possession of, and my lack of, that gift would have made me resentful and jealous at one time, but somewhere along the line, those children had sparked something in me.

For the first time in so long, I looked forward to getting up in the morning. I now had somewhere important to go and important people to see. I went to camp with growing warmth every day. The kids loved me, needed me. They wanted me there. If I quit, they would be disappointed. I knew how disappointment felt. It was dark and ugly and cold. They had saved me; the least I could do was not let them down. I now knew why I was here.

One day my group sat in a circle and sang along to a tape of the song "That's What Friends Are For." Jeni was at my side, and halfway through the song she began whispering questions.

"Lisa, have you heard this song before?"

"Yes."

"Do you think it's pretty?"

I dropped my arm around her shoulder, and we swayed back and forth to the music.

"Yes, Jeni, I think it's beautiful."

"Lisa, are you my friend?"

"Of course I am."

"Lisa, do you love me?"

I wiped away a tear that fell on my cheek.

"Yes, Jeni, I think I do."

Friends broaden our horizons. They serve as new models with whom we can identify. They allow us to be ourselves—and accept us that way. They enhance our self-esteem because they think we're okay, because we matter to them. And because they matter to us—for various reasons, at various levels of intensity—they enrich the quality of our emotional life.

JUDITH VIORST

I'll Never Forget You...Bardy

BY MARILYNN CARLSON WEBBER

I first met her at a church picnic at a time when I was feeling lost. We'd just moved to Seattle and it seemed that all the people in Carkeek Park knew one another and felt included—except me. So I was pleasantly surprised when an older woman purposefully made her way over to sit and talk to me. She was tall and vivacious, with silver hair and a touch of a Swedish accent. "My name is Gertrude Bardarson," she said, "but my friends call me Bardy." She was genuinely interested in what I had to say and she laughed often as she spoke. When at the end of the conversation she said, "I'm sure we'll be great friends," I felt she meant it.

If ever I needed a friend, that was the time. My husband, Bill, my widowed father-in-law, Dewey, and I had just moved that July from Springfield, Missouri, our home of ten years. It wasn't our first move, but it was certainly the hardest. For the first time I felt I lacked the energy to start over.

To be honest, it didn't make things easier that Dewey had moved with us. He could no longer drive, and I foresaw hours of chauffeuring him back and forth to town. Now he was sitting over with the older folks. He wasn't doing much talking. This move was hard on him too.

Later that week Bardy called. She asked if we could come to dinner on Tuesday night, a night never to be forgotten.

Her home was warm and inviting. It was hard not to notice a large painting, with swirls of color...and rocks. "From a Swedish painter," she explained. "Striking, don't you think? And guaranteed to be a conversation starter."

In fact, there was an array of intriguing artifacts around the homey living room, each with a story Bardy was happy to tell. But she was even more interested in finding out about us. There was something about Bardy that made me feel we had a great deal in common. We later discovered this is her natural way, as is turning friends of hers into friends of one another.

Bardy had prepared her specialty, salmon. She laughingly apologized that she hadn't caught it in Alaska herself, as she liked to do. The care she took in serving it made it look like a page from a gourmet magazine.

As I helped her clear the table, I was surprised to hear myself confiding in her. "It seems like last week that the kids were home, and I could stop by my mother's for coffee and conversation," I said sadly. "But now the kids are on their own, my mother died last summer and our friends are thousands of miles away. It just isn't what I'd hoped for at this time of life."

I caught myself as we reached the kitchen. "I'm sorry," I said. "You've lived here for so many years and have so many friends; I don't know if you can understand."

But her eyes were sympathetic. "Oh, Marilynn, I do understand. Even better, I know a secret, taught me by my immigrant mother. You see, she came over from Sweden, away from family and friends, to an arranged marriage. My parents weren't suited to each other. It's fair to say the marriage was not what my mother had hoped. Yet she lived a full and happy life—happy of her own choosing.

"Mother told me her secret at a low point in my own life," Bardy said, "but my sadness was the opposite of hers. I married a wonderful man. I felt like a schoolgirl each time I saw him coming home from work. He became the superintendent of schools in Carmel, California. Several years after we'd moved there, he kissed me good-bye one morning and went to work. I never dreamed before the day was over I'd be a widow. He died of a heart attack. He was only thirty-three."

After his death Bardy became very ill, even wondered if she wanted to go on living. Being a widow with two small sons was not what she'd hoped for.

"It might sound funny at first, but this is what my mother told me: Create your own party. Instead of moaning about the bad hand life has dealt you, be thankful for what you do have, and share it with those around you. You see, creating blessings for others in turn blesses you. You don't need to wait for a special day. For example, tonight I could have been home alone. But it's so much more fun to reach out and make new friends. There's always fulfilling work to be done, and new friends to make."

I told Bardy that I needed to return to work but was hesitant because I hadn't taught for ten years. To meet the requirements of a new state meant I'd need additional schooling. "I'm not sure I can do it. After all, I'm not as young as I used to be."

"Create your own party doesn't just mean parties!" Bardy said with a wink as she brought out dessert. "It means don't let yourself be sidelined." She explained she'd always wanted to be a registered nurse—so she went back to school and became one when she was sixty-three years old. "The real fun started when I graduated," she recounted. "When I applied for jobs, I was told, 'We retire people at your age, Mrs. Bardarson, we don't hire them.'"

So Bardy told God that if He didn't want her sidelined, He'd have to help her find her niche. That's when she was hired as a nurse by a retirement home. She was an instant hit with the residents. When they talked to her about their aches and pains, they found a sympathetic ear. After all, she had many of those aches and pains herself.

When her health no longer allowed her to work on the nursing floor, she began traveling as a nurse with blind tourists. "I'm getting to go to all the places I've always wanted to see," she reported as she served dessert.

I thought about Bardy's life all that week. If she could refuse to be sidelined in her sixties, surely I could go back to work in my forties. I sent for information on becoming a certified teacher in Washington State.

As Bardy predicted, we did become great friends. That winter at her annual Lucia Fest, the Swedish festival of lights that honors St. Lucia, fishermen swapped stories with university professors, while people from retirement homes reminisced with department store magnates. Somehow everyone fit together. As the years went by, I can't count the times I overheard her say at a church coffee hour, "Come on home with me for lunch. We'll see what I can whip up."

More than a decade has passed since that Tuesday dinner. Bardy is now in a nursing home; I've heard she's a favorite with the nurses, because she can sympathize with them. Bill and I have moved twice since then. After teaching for a while, with Bardy's encouragement, I started a new career as a public speaker. I want to pass along the thought that life should not be a matter of dwelling on your losses, but of counting your blessings, then purpose-fully reaching out to share them with others. As Bardy's mother taught her, and she taught me, this isn't an ability that a few people are born with; it's a "secret" available to all.

"You see, creating blessings for others in turn blesses you."

When I think of those early days of knowing her, I always remember when Dewey approached me apolo-getically the week after that first dinner at Bardy's. "Marilynn, I'm sorry to bother you, but could you take me into town for the Sixty-plus Group meeting at the church?"

"Sure, Dad," I said. Then a sly smile crossed my face. "But instead of taking you in for the meeting next week, why don't we have the folks here for lunch?"

I called Bardy to see if she'd give me a hand. The next week our kitchen bustled with people borrowing serving plates and sharing recipes. And there was Dewey in a circle of people, telling knee-slappers about the perils he'd faced as a World War I cook at Great Lakes.

"Thanks so much for inviting us over," said one vigorous woman as she helped straighten up the kitchen afterward. "It's been so good to get to know you."

"I'm sure we'll be great friends," I said sincerely.

Then I looked at Bardy, and we both smiled.

This is my commandment, that you love one another as I have loved you. Greater love has no one than this, that someone lay down his life for his friends. You are my friends if you do what I command you. No longer do I call you servants, for the servant does not know what his master is doing; but I have called you friends, for all that I have heard from my Father I have made known to you.

John 15:12-25

The Pitcher and the Preacher

BY BOB FELLER

I met Charlie Fix shortly after I hit the Big Leagues. At that time I was a green seventeen-year-old kid who had struck pay-dirt in big-time baseball.

Charlie Fix was a young minister—tall, lithe, clean-cut, and a straight thinker—from my own home town of Van Meter, Iowa. He had a small Methodist Church there. Charlie had been good at sports in high school and college, and I remember that it came as a surprise to me to discover that a reverend could be both a man of God and a good athlete.

Our friendship grew, and in years that followed our paths were to meet frequently. At the start of my first full year in baseball, I invited him to come down to spring practice with me at New Orleans.

At this time I was—as far as the experienced veterans of the Cleveland Indians were concerned—"damp" behind the ears. Frankly, they were pretty much right. For example,

I had been told that everyone in baseball chewed tobacco. Since my stomach couldn't take tobacco, I chewed licorice.

When I arrived in New Orleans in the spring with my "Preacher Friend," the older men on the squad were contemptuous. When they discovered that I had dug up a uniform for Charlie Fix, they really sounded off.

"We're such a bad influence on rookies that Feller has to bring his preacher on the field to keep us in line," one veteran growled sarcastically.

"Remember, fellas, no swearing now..."

"Oh, that would be orful..." came another in a high-pitched voice.

I listened with burning ears. I was worried too. Perhaps it all had been a bad idea.

The next day my worst fears were realized—some of the players were out to make Charlie look bad. Remarks were dropped at random to make him self-conscious... contempt in their faces.

Charlie was invited into a pepper game. This is a form of limbering up where one man taps out a ball to four or five players. Only the balls hit to Charlie could hardly be called taps. I noticed with pride that he more than held his own. He looked as lean, as agile and in as good condition as anyone else on the field.

Finally one leathery old vet picked up a ball and glove and motioned to Charlie that he wanted to "toss a few."

This pitcher—malicious and bad-tempered—was a bear on young players. From the smirks on the faces of the other players I knew there was dirty work afoot.

No one paid any direct attention to what followed, but I think everyone watched out of the corner of his eyes. The two began by throwing leisurely back and forth. Then the hard-skinned old pitcher started to put some stuff on the ball.

Smack came the crackling impact, and the young minister winced as he caught this scorcher. Charlie threw it back just as hard. A slow burn crept upon the old-timer's face. The young upstart! *Crack…crack…crack.* Back and forth the ball flew as the two tried to knock each other down. Charlie didn't budge an inch, although he was handling the fast balls of a famous pitcher nonchalantly with only a fielder's glove.

Finally, the manager noticed what was going on and rushed over angrily. "Cut it out," he bellowed at his star pitcher. "This is spring training, not mid-season."

But there was new respect for Charlie in the eyes of the players. And before the training season was over Charlie and the cantankerous pitcher were close friends. I was proud of him and glad that I had brought him down.

From then on, Charlie was a wonderful influence on me in so many ways. He never preached religion at me. To my questions about the church he gave straight-forward answers.

"Bob," he said to me once, "you know, I'd like to have you join my church—or any church, for that matter. But it's your decision. I think a lot of your friendship and I'm always ready to help you in any way that I can."

That hit home. At a time when organizations and people were really pushing me, Charlie simply offered friendship and help.

And just as he did at spring training that year, Charlie was always doing something to give stature and standing to the ministry. Everywhere he was winning the respect of those persons who had nourished the mistaken conception that ministers are stuffy, pompous, and physically inept.

We had just returned from a hunting trip one day to meet several reporters at the hunting lodge. As they crowded about with questions, I showed them my new rifle with a telescopic lens. Someone then placed a light bulb down the road a hundred yards or so. From where we stood it was just a small blob of light on a rock.

I gave the gun to the reporters and each tried it out. They shot holes in the nearby foliage and bounced bullets off the rock itself, but none came near the bulb.

"Give it a try, Charlie," I suggested. One of the reporters handed the gun to him gently and started to show him how to hold it, knowing that he was a clergyman. I chuckled to myself. Little did they know.

Charlie took a bead on the small white dot, pulled the trigger. There was a small tinkle and the light bulb dissolved. I looked with amusement at the surprised scribes, and chalked up another decision for Charlie.

Some time later I met Charlie in New York where we were playing an important series with the Yankees. In the first game the New Yorkers belted our pitcher hard to win, with Joe DiMaggio, their great outfielder, knocking out two home runs. Charlie viewed the game intently from a box that I had wangled for him.

"Know something," he said after the game, "that DiMaggio murders a high inside fast ball." I didn't pay much attention, and soon we were discussing other things.

The next day was my turn to pitch. In the first inning Joe DiMaggio came up. I worked the count around to two balls and two strikes. Then I wound up and poured in my fast ball—high and inside. Joe stepped back, took a hefty swipe at it, and I sadly watched the ball soar out of the park for a home run. Then I remembered Charlie's words of the day before.

In the ninth inning I had a slim one-run lead. When Joe DiMaggio came up again the crowd roared for him to duplicate his first inning home run to tie up the game. I fired in nothing but low inside pitches and struck him out to end the game.

I have to chuckle every time I think of how it took a minister sitting in the stands to pass on a tip to a ball player who had trained for years.

Then there was the time in Des Moines when I was to speak on a radio program. When I arrived at the station, a man from an advertising firm asked if I would endorse his product. "We'll give you five hundred dollars just for your name," he told me.

Five hundred dollars was a lot of money to me then, but I didn't use the product. "What should I do?" I asked Charlie. "Five hundred is easy money."

He smiled. "You never use the product?"

"I don't even like it," I answered. The decision was bigger than just a matter of money. Charlie knew it—and so did I. He wanted me to make the decision myself.

I went back to the advertising man and told him I couldn't use it.

Another decision came the same slow hard way. One Sunday morning in my home town my father, mother, sister and I went over to Charlie's Methodist Church together. It was the day for taking in new members.

At the given time I went forward and stood in front of my staunch friend. Solemnly I took the vows and accepted the responsibilities that go with church membership—vows that I will try my best to live up to every day of my life.

> *Walk with the wise and become wise, for*
> *a companion of fools suffers harm.*
>
> PROVERBS 13:20 (NIV)

The Blessings of Friendship

BY MARY ANN O'ROARK

Usually I talk about everything with my friends—that's what friends are for, right? But not my hip-replacement surgery. I guess I thought downplaying the whole thing would make it less scary. I kept telling myself I'd be fine. I could handle it on my own. Then my friend Mona and I were having one of our rambling conversations and I couldn't help myself. I blurted out the swiftly approaching date of my surgery. "How are you getting to the hospital?" she asked.

"I'll take the bus. It's not far."

"You are not going alone," Mona said. "I'm coming with you and I'm going to call Jeanne to see if she can come too." Jeanne, another dear friend.

The two of them picked me up at my apartment in a cab. They rode with me to the hospital and stayed. When I woke up in recovery, Mona and Jeanne were there. They helped me get settled in my room and gave me gifts that made me laugh—hot-pink feathers for my hair and cards with whimsical promises. ("This coupon entitles you to endless hours of your friends telling you how fabulous you are.") They distracted me from my pain and chased away my fears. My friends got me through something I thought I could endure on my own but now can't imagine it. And it wasn't the first time. Over the years, from my best friend in first grade, Karen Sue, to people I meet today, I've been blessed with many good friends. They've played a particularly important role in my life. Maybe because I'm single and don't have kids. But really, for any of us, friendship is a godsend. Just think of all the ways our friends are with us.

Friendship—my definition—is built on two things. Respect and trust. Both elements have to be there. And it has to be mutual. You can have respect for someone, but if you don't have trust, the friendship will crumble.

STIEG LARSSON

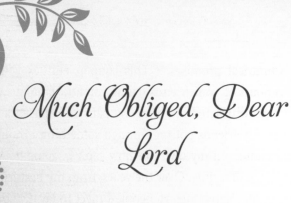

Much Obliged, Dear Lord

BY FULTON OURSLER

Her name was Anna Maria Cecily Sophia Virginia Avalon Thessalonians.

She was born into slavery on the Eastern Shore of Maryland, and her earthly master had thought it a great joke to saddle the little brown baby with that ungainly christening. As a young girl, in the first year of her freedom, Ann helped the doctor the day my mother was born. That was in 1866. Thirty-seven years later she was in the bedroom when I was born; she gave me my first bath, but that was not all she gave me.

I remember her as she sat at the kitchen table in our house; the hard old brown hands folded across her starched wrapper, the glistening black eyes lifted to the whitewashed ceiling, and the husky old whispering voice saying:

"Much obliged, dear Lord, for my vittles."

"Ann," I asked, "what is a vittle?"

"It's what I've got to eat and drink—that's vittles."

"But you'd get your vittles whether you thanked the Lord or not."

"Sure. But it makes everything taste better to be thankful. In some people's religion the whole family does it every meal. But not my church—I do it just for myself."

After the meal was over, she thanked the Lord again and then lit her clay pipe with reedy stem; to this day, every smoking pipe I smell makes me think of my old nurse.

"You know," she said, blowing expert rings in the direction of the kitchen range, "it's a funny thing about being thankful—it's a game an old colored preacher taught me to play. It's looking for things to be thankful for. You don't know how many of them you pass right by, unless you go looking for them.

"Take this morning, for instance. I wake up and I lay there, lazy like, wondering what I got to be thankful for now. And you know what? I can't think of anything. Tee-hee! What must the good God think of me, His child, but it's the honest truth—I just can't think of a thing to thank Him for.

"And then, what you think? My daughter, Josie, comes opening the bedroom door and right straight from the kitchen comes the most delicious morning smell that ever tickled my old nose. Coffee! Much obliged, dear Lord, for the coffee and the daughter to have it ready for an old woman when she wakes up. Much obliged, dear Lord, for the smell of it—and for the way it puts ambition even into me. Some people try to tell me coffee is bad, but I've been drinking it for fifty years now and I'm obliged to the dear Lord for every cup I get.

"Now for a while I've got to help Josie with the housework. It's a little hard to find anything to thank God for in housework; your ma will tell you the same thing and so will any other woman. But when I come to the mantelpiece to dust the ornaments, there's the Little Boy Blue. How long you think I've had that little china boy? Since before your mother was born. I was a slave when I got it for Christmas. But I never broke it; never even got it chipped. There he sits, all shiny blue, on the mantel, with his golden horn to his mouth. I love that little boy; he's been with me all the time; he's my little mantelpiece brother. Much obliged, dear Lord, for Little Boy Blue.

"And almost everything I touch with the dust rag reminds me of something I love to remember. Even the pictures that hang on the walls. It's like a visit with my folks, here and yonder. Funny, when you get to my age you've got as many of your folks up there as down here. The pictures look at me and I look at them and I remember so much that's good. I get through my housework before I know what I'm doing, I've been so busy remembering.

"You go downtown and look in the windows. So many pretty things."

"But Ann," I broke in. "You can't buy them. You haven't got enough money."

"I've always had enough money for what I want. I don't want those pretty things. What I want a long velvet gown for, trailing halfway behind? But I think it's pretty and I love to stand there and play dolls. Yes, I do. I play dolls in my mind, and I think of your ma, and your aunt Dot, and your cousin Leona, how each of them would look in that dress, and I have a lot of fun at that window. I'm much obliged to the dear Lord for playing in my mind, old as I am; it's a kind of happiness.

"Once I got caught in the rain. My daughter Josie thought I would catch my death. Tee-hee. It was fun for me. I always heard about fancy people's shower baths. Now I had me one and it was wonderful. So many things are wonderful. That cool water dropping on my cheeks was just exactly like a baby's fingers—and I always loved them.

"You know, God just is giving heaven away to people all day long. I've been to Druid Hill Park and seen the gardens, but you know what? I likes the old bush in your backyard a sight better. One rose will fill your nose with all the sweetness you can stand . . . ."

Now Ann must have told me these things at different times, but they have ranged themselves in my memory as one long, huskily whispered monologue. For a long while I forgot that she had ever said them.

It was not until trouble had clamped down on me with a throttlehold and my old ego had been battered. An hour came when I recognized danger in my own sense of despair. I searched my memory as a bankrupt frantically pokes through safety boxes, looking for a morsel of counsel. Ann had been a long time moldering in her grave, but her rumbling half-whispered tones came back to me, with the game she taught me at the kitchen table of searching out every cause for thankfulness.

I urged myself to play that game . . . I was in the subway at the time, which was vile-smelling and overcrowded—and it happened there was a burst of laughter that, probably because I was seeking it, reminded me that sorrow passes . . . and I looked about me and marked a young girl's eyes shining with hope for the evening; and again, pride in reading of a batsman's home run bringing glow to the face of a tired old clerk . . . and when I went up on the street, clean snow was falling; a church was lighted and its open doorway called to me. I went in. And I knelt. And my heart filled with warmth when I began to count over my many gifts, my many blessings—how much—how over-poweringly much I had to be grateful for.

For work to be done—good work that I could put my heart into—I'm much obliged, dear Lord, for that. For the ability to take care of those who looked to me. For my loved ones, who love me more than I deserve.

For friends; so many who had reached out or spoken, or who had mercifully kept silent in my troubles. And for utter strangers, whom I knew now God had sent to me in my trial, miraculously on hand to help...I found the words of thanks tumbling from my lips and heard myself thanking God even for difficulties because they renewed my faith....

There's magic in thanksgiving. You may begin with a cup of coffee, but once you start, the gratefulness swells and the causes multiply. Finally, it seems the more you thank the more you have, and the more you get, to be thankful for—and of course, that's the whole spiritual keystone.

The soul of long-dead Ann was a big soul, big enough to see God everywhere. I shall never be as big a soul as she was, but she taught me. The word came from the dingy street where she lived in East Baltimore, with Josie, her daughter, that Ann was dying. I remember Mother took me there in a cab. I stood by Ann's bedside; she was in deep pain and the hard old hands were knotted together in a desperate clutch. Poor old woman; what had she to be thankful for now?

She opened her eyes and looked at us; her eyes lingered with mine.

"Much obliged, dear Lord," she said, "for such fine friends."

She never spoke again—except in my heart. But there she speaks every day. I'm much obliged to God for that.

> *Setting an example is not the main means of influencing another, it is the only means.*
>
> ALBERT EINSTEIN

What Friendship Can Cost

AUTHOR UNKNOWN

Along about 1490, Albrecht Dürer and a young man known now only as Hans were struggling artist friends. They were very poor and had to work to support themselves while they studied. Work kept them from classes. Progress was slow. Then one day Hans, the older of the two, insisted that Albrecht devote all his time to study while he, Hans, worked to support them both. They agreed that when Albrecht was successful he would in turn support Hans, who would then learn to paint.

The bargain was struck. Albrecht went off to the cities of Europe to study painting. He had more than talent, it was genius, as the world now knows. He was soon successful and went back to keep his bargain with Hans. But Albrecht quickly discovered the price his devoted friend had paid. For Hans worked at manual labor, hard rough work, in order to support his friend. His slender, sensitive artist's hands had been ruined for life. Those stiff gnarled fingers could no longer use the artist's brush to make the delicate strokes necessary to painting. So Albrecht Dürer, great artist and great soul, painted the hands of his friend, painted them as he had so often seen them—raised in prayer for their success.

Today, art galleries throughout the civilized world still hold exhibitions of Albrecht Dürer's paintings and etchings. But of them all, beautiful and famous as they are, none holds the place in the hearts of the people as does *Praying Hands*, which tells its own eloquent story of love, labor, and sacrifice on the part of the subject, and of the love and gratitude of the painter.

> *One who has unreliable friends soon comes*
> *to ruin, but there is a friend who sticks*
> *closer than a brother.*
>
> PROVERBS 18:24 (NIV)

The Gift of Friendship

BY TERRI CASTILLO

The subway car screeched to a halt and an unusually cheerful voice piped: "Eighty-second Street, Jackson Heights—and Merry Christmas everyone!" Wrapping my scarf around my neck, I stared at the happy faces glowing under the bright subway lights. Women and children clung excitedly to colorfully wrapped boxes tied with shiny ribbons. Men chatted merrily, exchanging holiday greetings. The festive scene was unlike the usual somber subway rides. Tonight was Christmas Eve and the air was electric. For everyone, that is, but me.

This was my first Christmas in New York City. Leaving my family and friends back in Hawaii, I had moved here several months earlier—a young woman curious about the "Big City." It promised to be an exciting life, but it was sometimes a lonely one, and making friends wasn't easy. I'd hoped to spend the holidays with another young woman I had met in my apartment building, but she had been unexpectedly called home. Now, having no other friends nearby, I would spend Christmas alone.

As happy spirits escalated around me, I felt more and more homesick. "This is supposed to be a family celebration," I kept telling myself. "How can I celebrate Christmas without my family?" All I could think of was the empty room waiting for me, the television set my only company.

I slushed through the build-up of snow on the elevated platform and trudged down the icy steps leading to the street below. Strings of twinkling lights crisscrossed overhead along the avenue, forming arches of stars against the dark night. From the little shops lining the street, the sounds of Christmas carols floated through the air. I tucked my head under the hood of my coat to block out the sights and sounds around me. They only made me more homesick.

Light flurries of snow swirled against me as I quickened my pace. I'd soon be home. Crossing the street, I saw the big church on the corner. It was aglow with lots of candles burning brightly inside. A life-size crèche stood on the lawn with Joseph and Mary looking down at the Christ Child in the manger. A lighted sign next to it read: "Please join us for Midnight Mass on Christmas Eve." A tear slipped down my cheek. Midnight Mass was a tradition our family never missed. We always went to church together on Christmas

Eve. To go without them would only add to the pain I already felt. *Why*, I thought, *do I have to be six thousand miles from home this night?*

Inside the entranceway to my building I fumbled for my keys. Then I heard it. A soft, vaguely familiar voice singing: "Joy to the world, the Lord is come...." I stopped and looked around. No one was there. I listened curiously. "Let earth receive her King...." I poked my head out into the street. No one. I looked at the intercom unit on my right, and then I understood. The voice was coming from its speaker. Of course! It belonged to Mrs. Julia on the sixth floor. Mrs. Julia was a widow who lived alone in 6-B. She was a hearty soul who loved to stop residents in the lobby to chat—endlessly. More than once she'd told me more than I wanted to know about her herb garden and Felix, her housecat. Though she was a kind woman—she had brought me chicken soup one afternoon when she heard I had the flu—I had been avoiding her recently. I knew she was lonely, but I just didn't have the time to listen to her nonstop chatter. Now I could picture her sitting on the wooden stool next to the voice box in her kitchen, her wiry, silver hair tousled in a bun atop her head, singing to her neighbors as they came home.

As I listened, my body lightened. Her voice rang out: "Let ev'ry heart...prepare Him room...." The words awakened me like a splash of cold water on my face. Prepare Him room...

Why, this is what Christmas is about, I thought, *preparing room for Christ in my heart*. My mind raced back over the last few weeks. Had I prepared Him room? No, I hadn't. I had been too busy missing my family and friends. And in my loneliness I had closed my heart as tight as a clenched fist. To really celebrate Christmas meant I would have to open my heart—then I could make room for others. Maybe Christmas wouldn't have to be lonely after all . . .

Leaning against the intercom box, I drank in Mrs. Julia's radiant voice. "We wish you a Merry Christmas . . . we wish you a Merry Christmas . . . " she sang loudly. I pressed my finger on the button next to 6-B.

"Mrs. Julia," I said. "Mrs. Julia, this is Terri Castillo—down in 2-C."

"Merry Christmas, Terri!" she chimed back to me.

"Mrs. Julia," I said as a smile crossed my face, "how would you like to go to Midnight Mass with me tonight?"

> *Who hath a friend with whom to share hath double cheer and one half care.*
>
> AUTHOR UNKNOWN

You Can Help a Fallen Friend

I have always admitted that there was a God and believed in going to church. I sang in musical comedy and night clubs through the week and attended church every Sunday. But my liberal teaching didn't give me the true meaning of being a Christian. It isn't being good or a churchgoer that makes you a Christian. It's having Christ in your heart.

Lately I was well along Success Street, singing my way to stardom, yet my heart was black and I knew I was drinking myself into Failure Lane. Knowing I'd crack and lose everything—yet I couldn't quit.

Through friends, I had recently attended a Youth for Christ meeting with a group of young people from my home town, Norwalk, Connecticut, who were praying for me that I might use my voice for the Lord. They knew that I would be interested at least in the music. I was but couldn't join them in their "all-out salvation." They insisted that they wouldn't give me up but that they would continue to pray for me. They gave me a Gospel of John to read. At home I tossed it in a bureau drawer and the meeting was forgotten.

On May 9 one year I started to fill up with my quota of alcohol and to go through the usual Friday show at the night club. One of the patrons requested that I sing "On the Road to Mandalay." The words of that number, "Ship me somewhere east of Suez where the best is like the worst" were replaced in my wine-poisoned mind by others: "You want to know what I call sin? If I can't see Christ doing a certain something, that's sin."

Those words, which I'd heard the Saturday before (originally spoken by Hyman Appleman, world-famous evangelist) became such a mental torment that I could hardly finish my show.

At home I suffered all night. When I could think clearly, I asked my wife Helen to give me the Gospel of John. I opened it and read: "Verily, verily I say unto thee, except a man be born again, he cannot see the Kingdom of God" (John 3:5). For the first time in my life I knelt in true prayer. I told God that I didn't know what it meant to be born again, but that I wanted Him to show me.

It so happened that my friends asked me to sing for their Mother's Day evening service. I did. All the lights went out in the church toward the end of the sermon. The local powerhouse was inactivated for some reason, but the pastor finished his message in the dark.

My wife and I went home in the dark and I was standing by her as she lit a candle. No sooner had she lit it when the light bulbs came to full glow as the electricity was restored. In a second of absolute silence the Lord put a renewed light in my whole being. There was no doubt of my being reborn.

Last year, as tenor soloist for the Institute's Caroller Choir, I checked off almost every city where I had ever appeared when I was doing stage work. It was as if I went back on a pilgrimage.

But without the prayers of my friends I'd never have reached true faith. When reason and argument failed they didn't give me up—they set about to win me through prayer.

A faithful friend is a strong defense; and he that hath found him hath found a treasure.

LOUISA MAY ALCOTT

The Glory Crown

BY ANNE SIMPKINSON

One spring a couple years back, some colleagues and I were in Monroe, Louisiana, on business. We had plenty of time before our flight home, so we stopped for brunch. Between the main course and coffee, I slipped away to the restroom. I was walking through the restaurant, past other tables, when I noticed a statuesque African-American woman. She looked to be in her sixties and there was something so striking about her it was all I could do not to stare.

She was decked out in a lovely floral dress edged in lace. Atop her head was a hat with a profusion of lush and elegant blooms—roses, or maybe magnolias. A stunning Easter bonnet, even though it wasn't quite Easter yet. But more than what she wore, I was struck by how she held herself—with a grace that only age, experience, and wisdom can confer.

The strangest impulse hit me. *Stop and tell her how beautiful she looks in that hat.* But I caught myself. There was a teenage girl sitting next to her at the table and a middle-aged man opposite them—probably her son and granddaughter. I couldn't intrude on people I didn't know, and on a family meal, no less.

The feeling persisted, but I talked myself out of it. *She'll think you're crazy*, I told myself.

So I kept walking. On the way back to my table, I passed the woman again, and again I didn't say a word.

But when I saw her a third time, with her granddaughter in the parking lot after brunch, I couldn't help myself. I blurted out, "I have to tell you. Your hat is beautiful. And you wear it so well!"

"Why, thank you," she replied.

It felt good to say that, I thought, heading to my rental car. Just as I was backing out of my parking space, I heard someone shouting, "Ma'am! Ma'am!"

I looked back. The woman and her granddaughter were waving frantically at me.

Did I drop something when I stopped to talk to them? I turned off the engine, got out, and walked back to them.

"I'd like to give you my hat," the woman said.

"Oh no, I couldn't take your hat," I protested.

"My grandmother always taught me that if someone wanted what I had, I should give it to them," she said firmly.

Truth was, I didn't really want her hat. I just loved the way she looked in it. I hardly ever wear hats.

The woman looked at me expectantly, and it occurred to me that this wasn't about the hat. This was a gift being offered by a stranger, an act of generosity for which there was only one response.

"I will accept your hat," I said, "if you will be so kind as to place it on my head." Just like the compliment, the words came effortlessly.

The woman nodded. Then, with her granddaughter standing beside us, beaming, she lifted the hat off her head and slowly set it on mine. Her movements were so regal I felt as if she were crowning me with roses.

We threw our arms around each other and hugged, strangers no more.

"Thank you," I told her. "You have such a big heart."

"You have a big heart too," she said.

The walk back to my car had a ceremonial Easter parade feel to it. I waved to the woman and her granddaughter and drove off to the airport.

I wore the hat through security, all the way to my gate, and onto the plane. I didn't take it off until I was settled in my seat. That's when I noticed the tag inside the band. It read, "Glory Crown."

Back home, I Googled the words. They were from chapter four of Proverbs: "[Wisdom] shall give to thine head an ornament of grace: a crown of glory shall she deliver thee." How fitting! Once I had the wisdom to cast aside my inhibitions and trust the urge to compliment a stranger, I was graced with a crown of glory.

Open your heart. . . . Open it wide;
someone is standing outside.

MARY ENGELBREIT

"Is It I, Lord?"

I stalked across the hallway into my friend Ella's office. I had to vent about Debbie and what a royal pain she was being—to me, her boss, of all people! I was in my first year as chair of a technical college's English and social sciences department. If I'd told Debbie once I'd told her a dozen times that I needed her to rewrite her syllabus to emphasize essay writing rather than grammar rules. Why was she being so stubborn about completing this assignment? It bordered on insubordination!

"I don't think she's even started," I said, slumping into the seat across the desk from Ella, a fellow department chair and one of many people I'd sounded off to about Debbie. By now I didn't even have to tell her who I was talking about. "It's been weeks. I don't know what else I can do."

Ella looked up from the papers on her desk. "I know, Jayne. You've told me."

"I don't know what her problem is," I said. "She just doesn't listen. She's worse than my kids the way she defies me."

Ella looked back down, like she was studying something intently.

"She knows how important it is," I went on. "The university won't accept our credits otherwise. Then the other day I heard she was complaining to another instructor about me. As if I'm the problem! She's totally unprofessional. Now the faculty are taking sides. It's affecting the whole department."

Ella shook her head but didn't look up. She was probably tired of my complaining, but I didn't know where else to turn. It was all I could think about. Even at home when I tried to concentrate on prayer, my mind filled with frustration and anger. How dare Debbie treat me like this!

I stood up. "I'm going to talk to her again," I said. "But I doubt it will do any good." I left and walked slowly down the hallway to Debbie's office, the last place I wanted to be on a Friday afternoon. What did we have to say to each other that hadn't already been said?

I'd taught psychology for fifteen years. I thought I knew a lot about what makes people tick. But I never dreamed management would be like this. Even my husband, Frankie, who'd managed an auto-service department for years, was no help. I regaled him every night with my latest Debbie story, but I wasn't sure he could relate. In seventeen years of marriage I'd never heard him complain about a problem employee.

The worst part was that before I became department head Debbie and I were close colleagues. She'd been one of the first to congratulate me on my promotion. We had eaten lunch together occasionally, shared our work frustrations and news about our families. I'd tried to be a comfort when she lost her dad to cancer and when her mom became ill. Couldn't she see that she just needed to get this project out of the way?

I looked in her office. Her lips pressed tight together when she saw me. "Do you have a minute?" I said.

She opened her mouth, as if she were about to say something, then closed it and shrugged. "A minute," she said, not bothering to put her pen down.

I sat and her eyes fixed on mine. "You know why I'm here," I said. "I need you to get this assignment done for me. It's way past due and now the dean's asking about it. I can't keep covering for you."

"I'm working on it," she said. "I just need a little more time."

My hands clenched. The same lame response! "Debbie, you can't keep putting this off," I said, my voice rising. "You know how critical this is for the college and how important it is to me. It can't wait any longer."

Debbie threw her pen down. "You don't understand," she said. "You've never taught English. You're asking me to change my entire way of teaching."

I stood up. "You need to get control of yourself," I said. "I'm tired of your excuses." I turned and stormed out, my heart pounding. The nerve of her! I went back to my office and took out a legal pad to plan for the following week, but it was impossible to concentrate. I'd bent over backward for her, given her more than enough time. Maybe I wasn't an English teacher, but I'd certainly written enough syllabi to know it shouldn't be that difficult. Soon, in the eyes of the dean, I was going to be the problem. After all, I was Debbie's boss. Why couldn't I get her to do what I asked?

Frustrated, I stuck my legal pad in my satchel and left the office. I'd have to finish planning over the weekend. I hated taking work home, but I'd been so focused on Debbie I hadn't gotten anything done. My back felt like coiled springs being twisted tighter and tighter.

Over dinner I unloaded my frustration on Frankie and the kids. "You'll never believe what she did today," I said. "She actually threw a pen on her desk while I was talking to her."

Frankie looked over at me. "Can you pass the potatoes, please?" he said.

"I don't know how she thinks she can get away with treating me like that."

"Jayne," Frankie said, "would you mind passing the potatoes?"

"Here," I said, handing the bowl over. "I'm sorry. I'm just at my wit's end."

"Have you tried asking her why this is so difficult for her?" Frankie said.

"Yes," I said. "I've talked until I'm blue in the face. What more can I say?"

"I'm not sure," he said. "But clearly there's a communication problem."

My teenage daughters and nine-year-old son were talking about something across the table. "Will you be quiet?" I said. "I can't hear myself think."

Everyone around the table went silent. I didn't feel like eating. Frankie and the kids picked at their food too. Usually dinners were full of laughter, everyone sharing stories from their day. But lately our conversations had been strained. It certainly wasn't making my problems at work any easier to deal with.

That night in bed I said a silent prayer: *I've done everything I know how, Lord. Please help Debbie with this challenge.* I'd asked God before for help, but I knew any change was going to have to come from Debbie first.

I brooded all weekend. Sunday night I was in the living room, working on my to-do list for the week: complete the fall schedule of classes, hire adjunct faculty, plan a staff orientation meeting...

Frankie came in the room and laid a magazine article on the couch next to me. "I thought this might have some useful information for you," he said.

I glanced down at the headline: Marriage—Surviving Life's Stormy Seas. Why was he giving me this? Frankie and I didn't have any problems. We had been married so long we could finish each other's sentences.

I read further. The article related the biblical story of Jonah, how his stubborn actions threatened the lives of everyone around him on the ship that day. "Deep inside, Jonah knew he was to blame," I read, "but he didn't want to face it until it was nearly too late. Finally he asked, 'Is it I, Lord?'" I thought about the past few weeks and the squall growing around me. I'd spent more time talking about Debbie than with her. Our feud had embroiled other faculty members. It had spilled over to my family too. I was consumed with anger, snapping at my children. *Is it I, Lord?*

Frankie had asked me why Debbie was struggling with this task. I didn't know. I'd been dead-set on getting Debbie to listen to me. But I hadn't once tried to hear her.

I went back to my to-do list, crossed out the top item, and wrote: Meet with Debbie. I couldn't go any further without asking her to forgive me.

The next morning I went to her office before I even turned on my computer. Debbie looked up when I knocked on her door and I saw her body tighten.

"There's something I need to tell you," I said. "I'm sorry. I know this change is difficult for you and I haven't made it any easier. Please forgive me. If you have a moment I thought you might have some ideas on how we could do it better."

The tension in Debbie's face melted away. Two simple words was all it took. Why had it been so hard for me to say them? To simply ask for forgiveness? I sat down across the desk from her, now more a bridge than a barrier.

"Let me show you what I've done," she said. "I was thinking that I would start out by having my students write an essay."

"That sounds great," I said.

"I'm sorry it has taken me so long," Debbie said. "I know we both want what's best for the students." We talked for a few more minutes. I asked about her mother and she about my kids. Then I stood, walked around her desk, and hugged her. There was a connection, a unity of purpose, and a peace I knew could only come from God. The storm had lifted.

The next time I had a disagreement with a colleague, I wouldn't let it escalate. Like Jonah, I'd ask, "Is it I, Lord?" Then I would listen.

The difference between holding on to hurt or releasing it with forgiveness is the difference between laying your head at night on a pillow filled with thorns or a pillow filled with rose petals.

LOREN FISCHER

The Angel Factory

BY BOBBIE BURNETT

My garage is overflowing with cardboard boxes. Stacks of storage containers line my spare bedroom and foam packing pellets are scattered all over the basement. Am I moving? No. But I've been moved. By angels.

Thirty years ago, my husband, Jerry, an electrical engineer, got a job in Annapolis. We bought a house here and one of the first people I met was Susie—a bright, energetic, witty mom of three. We belonged to the same women's organization. Spending time with Susie, I forgot I was new in town. She made me feel so at home.

But our carefree days were cut short. Just before Christmas one year Susie was diagnosed with leukemia. She started chemotherapy treatments right away at Johns Hopkins oncology center in Baltimore. I called her often, wrote her little get-well cards, and visited her in the hospital. Then another setback: Her husband was laid off. "I'm so worried about all the medical bills piling up," she confided during one visit. "Can you please pray for us?"

So I did. Every day. But I wanted to do more. Friends of ours shuttled her kids to after-school activities, others cooked meals and baked desserts. Now, as Jerry can attest, I'm no cook. I am an artist, though. One night, lying in bed, I tossed and turned. *Lord, help me use my art to help Susie.* My mind drifted to a stained-glass class I'd taken a while back. I usually worked with oil paints, but there was something about the way sunlight shimmered through the glass that felt peaceful, almost healing.

What else was peaceful and healing?

Angels.

The next morning I got right to work. I used an aqua shade of glass (Susie's favorite color) for the body and a silvery pearl glass for the wings. It was a long, painstaking process—lining up the pattern, cutting the glass, foiling the sides. I worked a little bit at a time. Susie's angel stood just over a foot tall, and I topped her off with a golden halo and added a holder for a votive candle.

A couple of days before Christmas, I brought the angel to Susie's hospital room. "I made this for you," I said.

"Oh, Bobbie!" Susie gasped. "I love it! Put her on the table over there so I can see her all the time."

Whenever I'd visit Susie, she'd tell me how much she loved the angel. I thought she was just being sweet. One afternoon, though, she mentioned that someone had asked her where they could buy one. "I told them you made it for me," she said. "And they asked me where you sell them. You really ought to make more of these."

More? I loved making the angel—but it had taken me almost twenty hours. There was no way I'd have the time to make more and keep up with my other artwork. I was about to tell Susie it was impossible when it hit me: I'd round up the folks who asked her about the angel and teach them how to make one too. Then we could sell them and give the money to Susie and her family to help with her medical expenses.

I invited about a dozen women—mostly Susie's friends and family—over to my house. Right there in my living room, we cut shapes from sheet glass and wrapped the edges in foil. Even Jerry got in on the act, helping us solder the pieces together. I told Susie about our stained-glass operation. She was thrilled! Within a few months we presented her family with a check for two hundred dollars. It wasn't much, but it was a start.

Word of mouth spread...fast. Soon we had thirty volunteers and an assembly line that outgrew our living room. Jerry and I cleared the clutter out of our basement and set up shop down there. "It really looks like an angel factory!" Jerry said, laughing, when he saw all of us at work.

A year after we started making angels we'd raised more than a thousand dollars for Susie and her family.

Despite aggressive treatment, her health grew worse. On December 15, a year after she was diagnosed, Susie died.

Heartbroken, we donated the rest of the profits to Susie's doctor, who was conducting leukemia research. Several months later, Susie's husband and parents urged us to make more angels. A lot more. They wanted the money to go to area hospitals so even more folks could benefit. It was a great idea, but I was worried. Selling a few angels to help Susie was one thing. Would we be able to sell enough to help hundreds, maybe thousands, of patients and doctors? That afternoon I stood and looked around—at the hardworking volunteers, the assembly line. The Angel Factory. I closed my eyes. *Lord, I'm putting this in Your hands. Show me what to do with these angels.*

Almost immediately the phone rang. It was a woman calling from Oregon. "I heard about your angels from a friend of mine who lives in Maryland," she said. She placed an order for ten of the larger stained-glass angels—they were forty dollars each! From then on it seemed like the orders never stopped coming. Susie's family was right—the angels were a hit! I put aside my artwork to make angels full time.

Ten years later we were officially a nonprofit. We called ourselves Caring Collection, Inc., and added other stained-glass figurines, angel pins, and sun catchers in every shape from hummingbirds to lighthouses. Orders from all over the world poured in: France, Germany, England, Russia, Australia, South Africa. It seemed everyone had been touched by cancer. People really wanted to help.

And they still do! To date we've donated $845,000 for cancer-research equipment to the Johns Hopkins oncology center, where Susie was treated, and for patient-care equipment to the Anne Arundel oncology center in Annapolis. We've helped the hospitals purchase ultrasound machines, blanket warmers, and fiber-optic devices that detect tumors. Our goal is to raise one million dollars—and I know we'll reach it.

A few major corporations have offered to mass-produce the angels over the years, but I've turned them down. Part of what makes these figurines so special is that each one passes through the caring hands of more than twenty of our volunteers before it's finished. I think each angel carries all that love and hope to the recipient. Susie would be proud of that.

These days my basement is more crowded than ever. Jerry and I don't have children, but our ninety volunteers make a big extended family. Let me make it clear, though, that these workers don't come around for free. Oh no. We pay them . . . in jelly beans and pretzels!

Our youngest is a fourteen-year-old high-school student. Our oldest? An eighty-nine-year-old retired teacher. Each volunteer has her own story, his own reason for being part of the Angel Factory. Some are cancer survivors, some are undergoing treatment, and some just want to help because they can. Like Katherine, who started volunteering when she was still in high school. Back then she cut her fingers more than she cut the glass! Now she cuts our patterns like a pro and is teaching me how to use the computer.

Then there's Sylvie. I met her around the time I started making the angels. Some of my artwork was going to be displayed in a gallery in the South of France. I had two weeks to learn some French, so I called a local language organization. Sylvie answered. "You're not going to learn much in two weeks," she said. And you know something? She was right. I still can't speak a lick of French, but in those two weeks I told Sylvie so much about the angels that she's been volunteering ever since.

Perhaps the three most fervent supporters of the Caring Collection are a dedicated set of siblings whose lives have been forever altered by cancer: Susie's children, Katie, Jenny, and Matt.

I've had people ask me, "Do you think you'll ever stop making angels?" The truth is, I almost did. When Jerry retired he said, "Please retire with me. You've spent years making these angels, and they've helped a lot of people. But maybe it's time for a break. Just think of all the trips we can take."

I had to admit, seeing the world together sounded enticing. But several months after he retired, Jerry was diagnosed with colon cancer. His prognosis was good, yet I couldn't help but worry. To lift his spirits I did the best thing I knew how: I made him a stained-glass angel. *If I retire, this could be the last angel I make,* I thought, hanging it from the IV pole in Jerry's hospital room. Jerry looked at the angel, then at me. Tears filled his eyes.

"Promise me you'll never stop making these," he said. "Everyone needs an angel. Everyone needs hope."

Jerry's now in remission and his angel hangs on our living-room wall—a reminder to keep the Caring Collection going for as long as we possibly can.

See what I mean when I said I've been moved by angels?

I think if I've learned anything about friendship, it's to hang in, stay connected, fight for them, and let them fight for you. Don't walk away, don't be distracted, don't be too busy or tired, don't take them for granted. Friends are part of the glue that holds life and faith together. Powerful stuff.

JON KATZ

My Prayer Partner

BY JAMIE HOWARD

I stared at my reflection. The bald, hollow-eyed woman in the mirror looked so tired and sad, nothing like a young wife and mom with her whole life ahead of her. Maybe it was because I couldn't quite trust that I had a future after being stricken with breast cancer at thirty-three. Even though my surgery and treatment were behind me, I was unable to shake the fear and hopelessness. I wanted to pray but couldn't quiet my mind enough to find the words. I called my old college roommate, Christine Hutchens. "Will you be my prayer partner?" I asked.

She didn't hesitate, even when I explained she'd be doing all of the praying. "I've been wanting to do something for you," Christine said. "I'll call you every morning at six forty-five." And she did, no matter how busy she was getting ready for work or her kids off to school.

For a while, all I could do was close my eyes and listen while Christine talked to God for both of us. Slowly I grew stronger and joined in, surrendering my burdens to God and thanking Him for my blessings.

Four years later, my faithful friend Christine and I still pray together every morning. No wonder when I look in the mirror now, I see a woman glowing with health, with joy in the present and hope for the future.

> *So take another breath for now, and let the tears come washing down, and if you can't believe I will believe for you.*
>
> STEVEN CURTIS CHAPMAN

My Two Best Friends

BY BROCK HIBBS

I have a seizure disorder, ADHD, and a hearing impairment—all of which made me a prime target for bullies. Kids loved to make fun of me. Finally my mom had enough and enrolled me in a new school, Peaster Independent, Peaster, Texas, in eighth grade.

That first day at Peaster, I was nervous. Scared. I walked into homeroom and stood in the back. Suddenly two guys walked up. *Here it comes,* I thought.

"Hi, my name's Jon," one of the boys said. "I'm Tommie," said the other. Soon we were talking about sports, favorite subjects in school, even girls.

Jon and Tommie stuck by me over the years. They supported me when I joined the prom committee, asked me to be the manager for our high school baseball team, even helped me meet the girl I liked.

"You can do anything you want," Jon would say.

He was right. I overcame the odds, eventually graduating from Peaster High. Now I'm in my last semester of college, pursuing a degree in early childhood education. I hope to pass the courage my two best friends gave me to kids who have struggles like mine. I want them to know they too can succeed.

> *Surround yourself with "yay-sayers"*
> *not naysayers.*
>
> LYNN A. ROBINSON

Oil and Water

BY JUDI LONGFELLOW

*O*il and water, that's us, I thought when I met Teri twenty years ago. She was outspoken. I'm reserved. Teri didn't wear makeup; I wouldn't leave home without it. Back in the day, Teri loved hitting the road on her Harley. I preferred curling up with a good book. *We're just so different,* I thought.

Until I went through a devastating divorce. I passed the days in a fog, sobbing for hours when I got home from work. Friends and family called, worried. A phone call wasn't enough for Teri. One day she strode into my office. "You need to have some fun," she said. "I'm taking you to a Garth Brooks concert this weekend."

"I can't," I protested. "I'm not ready to go out." But Teri wouldn't take no for an answer. We had a blast at the concert! For the first time in ages, I laughed and felt like life could go on. Soon Teri and I were going to more concerts, San Diego Chargers football games, church volunteer projects. One day I gave Teri a card. "Thank you for never giving up on me," I wrote.

Slowly I climbed out of that terrible darkness, in large part because of Teri, who boldly showed me that life is full of joys—especially our friendship.

> *A friend is one who strengthens you with prayers, blesses you with love, and encourages you with hope.*
>
> AUTHOR UNKNOWN

A Note from the Editors

We hope you enjoy *Stories of Friendship to Warm the Heart*, created by the Books and Inspirational Media Division of Guideposts, a nonprofit organization. In all of our books, magazines and outreach efforts, we aim to deliver inspiration and encouragement, help you grow in your faith, and celebrate God's love in every aspect of your daily life.

Thank you for making a difference with your purchase of this book, which helps fund our many outreach programs to the military, prisons, hospitals, nursing homes and schools. To learn more, visit GuidepostsFoundation.org.

We also maintain many useful and uplifting online resources. Visit Guideposts.org to read true stories of hope and inspiration, access OurPrayer network, sign up for free newsletters, download free e-books, join our Facebook community, and follow our stimulating blogs.

To learn about other Guideposts publications, including our best-selling devotional *Daily Guideposts*, go to ShopGuideposts.org, call (800) 932-2145 or write to Guideposts, PO Box 5815, Harlan, Iowa 51593.